The Making of a Musical

Lehman Engel

LIMELIGHT EDITIONS

NEW YORK

Library of Congress Cataloging-in-Publication Data

Engel. Lehman, 1910–
    The making of a musical.

    Reprint. Originally published: New York: Macmillan, c1977.
    Includes index.
    1. Musical revue, comedy, etc.—Writing and publishing.
    2. Musical revue, comedy, etc.—Production and direction.
    I. Title.
    MT67.E6 1985   782.81   85-18148
    ISBN 0-87910-049-4 (pbk.)

To the members of my
BMI Musical Theatre Workshops

NEW YORK

LOS ANGELES

TORONTO

past and present—
with love

ACKNOWLEDGMENTS

The author wishes to acknowledge the invaluable assistance of Jed Mattes and Mitch Douglas in the preparation of this manuscript.

Contents

Contents

x

Introduction

IN ALL COUNTRIES, theatre in some form has existed at all times. In most instances it has sprung from religious celebration and has seldom been without music.

The place of music in the theatre is our chief concern here. From the beginning, there was some kind of orchestra and a chorus. These preceded the use of the solo voice.

Western theatre probably began with the Greeks and continued on, though in a lesser degree, with Roman comedy and drama. The use of music was important to both. In medieval times, there were Mystery and Miracle plays written for and performed in the church, which employed both vocal and orchestral music. As the centuries passed, music became more vocal, drama became independent of religion, and comedy—which at first was a new element in theatre, separate from tragedy—became integrated with it.

Opera—a dramatic tale told in words with continuous

music—began about 1600 and evolved until, quite unintention-
ally, the music became more important than the words. This
kind of imbalance was to continue in a variety of different
ways through many centuries and right up to the present.

The musical (musical comedy, play with music, musical
show, etc.) evolved to its highest point in the United States
between 1927 and 1970. At first it grew out of operetta—Viennese especially—which had been born from opera itself. Although various forms of "light" stage musicals had existed
from at least the thirteenth century in all European countries,
this form was crystallized most notably in 1728 in England in
John Gay's *The Beggar's Opera*, a musical comedy containing
sixty-nine songs, all with new lyrics relevant to the play and
adapted to a wide variety of well-known music, including folk
songs, ballads of all kinds, and even music from a Handel
opera.

The Beggar's Opera was performed in America late in the
eighteenth century and inspired imitators; but numerous original "shows" began to emerge at about the same time. This
form of stage musical continued on throughout the nineteenth
century, when other forms, including burlesques, pan-
tomimes, extravaganzas, variety shows, vaudevilles, and minstrel shows, also were employed. All except minstrel shows
had origins in various other European forms that included
commedia dell'arte, ballet, etc.

Before the turn of the nineteenth century, we had witnessed
the importation of Gilbert and Sullivan's operettas from England, Offenbach's from France, Strauss' and Lehar's from
Vienna; but we had also begun simultaneously to create native
entertainments that, while owing a great debt to earlier European models, had nevertheless become something new, something not quite definable as European.

Even so, like a chameleon, the new version, the American
show, had many different colors. The works of John Philip

Sousa and Reginald de Koven were operettas that sometimes came perilously close to opera. A very short time later, Victor Herbert, attempting to perpetuate Viennese operetta, began creating a steady and significant series of shows that can only be classified as musical comedies. During the more than two decades that these composers occupied the American stage, a wide variety of revues successfully vied for patronage and grew in opulence and simplemindedness. Earlier examples are the shows of Harrigan and Hart (1879–1896), which were unvarnished, folk-like, family-type shows with a cultivated Irish brogue; and the Weber and Fields shows, which had a German flavor. The former relied more strongly on "original" songs, the latter on stars and comedy.

The opulent revues began around 1903 and grew under many aegises through the 1930s. The big ones—Ziegfeld Follies, Earl Carroll Vanities, The Passing Shows, Greenwich Village Follies, Music Box Revues, and others—relied on girls, scenery, costumes, and stars. Sometimes music was more than accompaniment, and occasionally dance was more meaningful than high kicks.

The large revue, however, played—unknowingly—an important role in the future of the American musical theatre when it provided opportunities for young writers such as Cole Porter, Irving Berlin, the Gershwins, and others to exhibit their wares.

But the splashy revues were phased out because the public tired of the large, larger, and largest vapidity and mindlessness (Ziegfeld ended in bankruptcy). While the big revues still struggled for survival, the road was divided into two *other* related, but quite different, offshoots.

The first of these represented a meaningful reaction against the biggest revues, and substituted ideas and satire for girls-for-their-sexual-attractiveness and production ornateness. These minimusical revues included the earliest Rodgers and

Hart successes, the *Garrick Gaieties* (1925 and 1926) and *The Grand Street Follies* (1924). Later, there were others in the same tradition, such as the series of Leonard Sillman's *New Faces* that began in 1934, and Harold Rome's *Pins and Needles* (1937). The other "turn" incorporated ideas and satire that had been notably absent from the large revues, but were themselves opulent in new ways, employing homogeneous scores— usually by a single composer-lyricist team as opposed to the previous mishmash of contributors—and omitting the girls-for-girls'-sake. Among these were *The First Little Show* (1929), *Three's A Crowd* (1930), *The Band Wagon* (1931), *Flying Colors* (1932), and *As Thousands Cheer* (1933), to name but a few.

In the process of evolution, there is constant reaction against the old, reversion to the still older in a newer guise, and an overlap involving what is passing and what is beginning. As the revues were being phased out, there was a return to the book show or musical comedy.

It is difficult to pinpoint the reasons for the demise of the literate revues, but one might venture more-or-less safe guesses. While the scores of these shows were distinguished new accomplishments by many of the leading writers in our native theatre (Rodgers and Hart, Schwartz and Dietz, Berlin, and many more), the shows seemed to lean most heavily on the comedy sketches provided by such top-drawer writers as George S. Kaufman, Heywood Broun, Howard Dietz, Moss Hart, and others. Their sketches assumed greater and greater importance, since they provided the comedy stars with what became their most memorable material and the audiences' chief delight.

With the passing of time, true humor became rare, as did the great clowns who performed it. Since much of what was most successful satirized everyday living, the government, headlines, big business, etc., there was an inescapable feeling of inhibition when the witchhunts of the Forties and Fifties began inquisitions of all "enemies"—a term synonymous with people of differing points of view. Fear and revulsion were successfully generated against many people in the entertainment industry—writers, performers, directors, and so on— and suddenly, there was an end to merriment. The freedom to satirize was fraught with dangers that intimidated (and for very strong personal reasons) the writers who had trafficked in it. The revue sketch under these conditions would have been emasculated. The writers were emasculated, the great clowns were phased out and they died, leaving no heirs.

Meanwhile—before, during, and after this period—the book-musical was evolving. Jerome Kern consciously worked toward the integration of book, music, and lyrics, and his efforts climaxed in *Show Boat* (1927). The Rodgers and Hart collaboration began two years earlier and came to maturity as musical theatre (the songs had always been extraordinary) with *Pal Joey* (1940). The Gershwins had reached their peak with *Porgy and Bess* (1935). Porter, Berlin, Schwartz-Dietz, Arlen, Styne, Lane-Harburg, Rome, and others made their marks in the newly developed musical in the Forties.

What were the chief differences between the earlier shows and those that emerged between 1927 and 1972? The earlier ones had—as shows—succeeded because of incredibly opulent collections of songs (they were not "scores," since their relationships to characters, situations, and to each other were peripheral), a sense of youthfulness, a feeling of lightheartedness, and stars who were made by, and continued to inhabit, the musical show world of that time.

On the other hand, the more mature musical has produced shows with more literate books, three-dimensional characters, and scores that characterize the singers, further the plot, and in themselves help to form a coherent entity. The fact that many of the scores seem less opulent than those earlier ones which contained songs more easily detachable from their shows is not due entirely to the quality and nature of the songs themselves, but to the fact that, in earlier shows, many songs were reprised again and again. Today—right or wrong—this practice has seemed old-fashioned, for the reprised songs were usually heard again for their own sakes rather than for the characters' or for their relevance to the progress of the show.

Of particular bearing here are some reasons for composer, lyricist, and librettist to consider the following pages:

The first point to be made is that, although the musical theatre in America is at present undergoing great transitions, the principles relevant to the realization of a successful, workable show have not changed basically. Nor are they apt to change. By this time, there have been so many memorable shows and so many more failures (many successes have been failures in the profoundest sense) that it is possible to deduce from them certain fundamentals that apply to the workableness of all shows. Hopefully, in the following pages these will be clearly indicated.

Second, when the twenties spawned the group of young men who were attempting to learn their trade as musical theatre writers, the production cost of a show, in comparison with the cost today, was so small and the number of productions therefore so great that new writers had many more opportunities than the new writers of our own time to learn by experience. The very revues that held the boards in profusion during the first quarter of the present century provided important stepping-stones for talented new creative people. Because the sketches, music, and lyrics were composed by an army of different writers, there was minimum responsibility for any one contributor, and producers could afford the risk of trying out a song by a new composer or a sketch by an unknown. A failed song, being easily and quickly replaceable, represented only a small threat to the whole project; a success provided a foot in the door for composer and lyricist, and was usually followed in a subsequent show by a fuller participation on the part of the new creative talent.

Thus, writers learned by experience and grew through participation. With these opportunities minimized today by the appearance of fewer shows, higher production costs, and ready availability of those who already possess a highly esteemed track record, newcomers, in order to minimize as far as possible the risk of failure, must exercise every precaution to learn their crafts in advance of an opportunity to participate professionally.

What follows is a step-by-step analysis of the elements that comprise a musical show. The reader interested in creating a musical is encouraged to write his own examples of each kind of song and scene under discussion.

This is the curriculum that the author has developed during more than a decade in the Musical Theatre Workshops established under the aegis of Broadcast Music, Inc. More and more members of these Workshops in New York, Los Angeles, and Toronto are being produced or are now moving forward in that direction. The only workshop ingredient necessarily lacking in this presentation is personal criticism of the participant's writing, and knowledgeable criticism and discussion are vital to every creative person's maturing. However, when the principles outlined in the following pages are sincerely, objectively, and intelligently integrated in the writer's own work, he must experience growth.

The author urges readers to refer in depth to the musical shows recommended here as examples of our theatre's highest achievements. A thorough understanding of these and an application of the principles espoused in this text should aid the writer considerably in achieving his aims.

The Music

FOR A MUSICAL show to succeed as an artistic entity (also, invariably, as a commercial one), all of its many collaborative parts must work together. The principal differences between *Carousel* and *Liliom* (Molnar's play on which the musical was based), between *West Side Story* and *Romeo and Juliet*, or *A Little Night Music* and Ingmar Bergman's film *Smiles of a Summer Night*, are the ways in which the original material was altered for the musical theatre stage, and the music-lyrics themselves. All of the other elements have their indispensable importance, but let us first consider only the music.

Musically, within a show, there is a kind of program consisting of several different classifications of music that follow along in a contrasting sequence. At the root of each—as different as one song may be from another—is the form which we call *A A B A*. This was not invented in the theatre but grew in similar forms in all Western music, including folk songs, symphonies, and the rest. There are frequent variants or multiples of this which I will demonstrate later, but now at the start let us content ourselves with understanding this basic form.

Each of these letters represents a musical block, each one usually of the same length. Each is most often eight measures long so that the *chorus*, or *refrain*, which is at the core of all songs, is ordinarily thirty-two bars—or four times eight.

In the theatre, this form has great advantages in that section *A*, which contains the main theme of the song, is heard three times. This gives the listener a better chance to remember it since, in hearing a single chorus, he hears this theme three times. The first *A* states it, the second *A* repeats it, usually leading at its end toward another key, a fact which will generally require some minor harmonic and melodic alteration.

The *B* section is known variously as the *release* or *bridge*, although in my own opinion *relief* is a more appropriate designation. This part almost invariably is, and should be, musically and lyrically in contrast to the *A* sections. There are innumerable ways in which this can be accomplished:

1. the note values of the two can be contrastingly of longer or shorter time values;

2. the key of the *B* section should be as different as possible;

3. the rhythm may contain less movement when *A* is jaunty (for instance), or it may contain more notes and *feel* faster, although the basic beat or tempo does not change.

(The lyric differences will be discussed later.)

After *B*, there is the return to *A* in its original state, finally progressing toward a satisfying ending for the entire chorus.

This *A A B A* form is to be found in the theatre music of all composers from the mid-nineteenth century to the present time. The simplest variation happens when the composer, in the case of a swiftly moving refrain, *doubles* the length of each section (blocks of sixteen measures instead of eight). In such cases, the proportions of the song remain unchanged and the chorus will become sixty-four bars long instead of thirty-two.

The following are a few random examples of the thirty-two-bar form:

"The Man I Love," by George and Ira Gershwin
"I Want to Be Happy," by Irving Caesar and Vincent Youmans
"Smoke Gets in Your Eyes," by Otto Harbach and Jerome Kern
"I'll Follow My Secret Heart," by Noël Coward
"September Song," by Maxwell Anderson and Kurt Weill
"Bewitched, Bothered and Bewildered," by Richard Rodgers and Lorenz Hart
"The Love of My Life," by Alan Jay Lerner and Frederick Loewe

The following are a few examples of the doubled-length refrain:

"The Most Beautiful Girl in the World," by Richard Rodgers and Lorenz Hart
"Wunderbar," by Cole Porter
"If Ever I Would Leave You," by Alan Jay Lerner and Frederick Loewe (16, 16, 8, 16)
"Just One of Those Things," by Cole Porter

Exceptions will be indicated nearer the end of this section.

Overeager, sometimes talented new composers may bristle at the very idea of the restrictive *A A B A* concept, but I would like to assure them that its virtues, partly listed before, far outweigh its limitations. Composers (or lyricists) have to express ideas as succinctly, as expressively, and as completely as possible, and, although the limitations of the *A A B A* form may repel some of them, they will find that practice of this simple form, *because* of its restrictions, will teach them to write in a more disciplined manner, and will help prevent them from writing in a sprawling, endless, formless style.

This *A A B A* form only applies to the chorus, or refrain. Especially in the theatre, the chorus is preceded by a *verse* or *introduction*, two names referring to the same first (or prerefrain) part of the song. There is no *single* accepted or recommended form or length for this verse section (the name I prefer). Generally, its length is determined by the extent of the idea which the composer and lyricist feel they need for a proper setup of their chorus.

The only factor which I feel ought to be pointed out is one involving contrast between the musical quality of the verse and that of the chorus. For example, if the verse begins too tunefully, the hearer may mistake it for the chorus, which should clearly be the "main event." Actually the verse, besides supplying a suitable setup to the ensuing refrain, should also behave in much the same way that a frame compliments a picture: one can never confuse the one with the other.

The following list of verses to songs demonstrates their diversity of length. When the reader listens to these, he should also note the musical contrast between these verses and their choruses.

> "Where Is the Life that Late I Led?" (Cole Porter) from *Kiss Me, Kate*—6 lines
>
> "I Get a Kick Out of You" (Cole Porter) from *Anything Goes*—7 lines
>
> "It's Delovely" (Cole Porter) from *Red, Hot and Blue*—13 lines
>
> "Here in My Arms" (Richard Rodgers and Lorenz Hart) from *Dearest Enemy*—8 lines
>
> "Blue Room" (Richard Rodgers and Lorenz Hart) from *The Girl Friend*—12 lines
>
> "Johnny One Note" (Richard Rodgers and Lorenz Hart) from *Babes in Arms*—1 line

"Spring Is Here" (Richard Rodgers and Lorenz Hart) from *I Married an Angel*—5 lines

"Ol' Man River" (Jerome Kern and Oscar Hammerstein) from *Show Boat*—4 lines

"The Surrey with the Fringe on Top" (Richard Rodgers and Oscar Hammerstein) from *Oklahoma!*—4 lines

"Lonely Room" (Richard Rodgers and Oscar Hammerstein) from *Oklahoma!*—6 lines

"Younger Than Springtime" (Richard Rodgers and Oscar Hammerstein) from *South Pacific*—8 lines

"Hello, Young Lovers" (Richard Rodgers and Oscar Hammerstein) from *The King and I*—12 lines

"Embraceable You" (George and Ira Gershwin) from *Girl Crazy*—10 lines

"Someone to Watch Over Me" (George and Ira Gershwin) from *Oh, Kay!*—14 lines

"I Got Rhythm" (George and Ira Gershwin) from *Girl Crazy*—12 lines

"Something to Remember You By" (Howard Dietz and Arthur Schwartz) from *Three's a Crowd*—10 lines

"Geisha" (Howard Dietz and Arthur Schwartz) from *At Home Abroad*—12 lines

"New Sun in the Sky" (Howard Dietz and Arthur Schwartz) from *The Band Wagon*—6 lines

"April in Paris" from *Walk a Little Faster* (E. Y. Harburg and Vernon Duke)—7 lines

"It's Only a Paper Moon" (E. Y. Harburg and Harold Arlen) from *The Great Magoo*—8 lines

"If I Only Had a Brain" (E. Y. Harburg and Harold Arlen) from *The Wizard of Oz*—5 lines

"I Can't Give You Anything but Love" (Dorothy Fields and Jimmy McHugh) from *Blackbirds of 1928*—8 lines

"I Feel a Song Coming On" (Dorothy Fields and Jimmy McHugh) from *Every Night at Eight*—4 lines

5

"I'll Buy You a Star" (Dorothy Fields and Arthur Schwartz) from *A Tree Grows in Brooklyn*—6 lines

"Nobody Makes a Pass at Me" (Harold Rome) from *Pins and Needles*—10 lines

"Chain Store Daisy" (Harold Rome) from *Pins and Needles* —26 lines

"Welcome Home" (Harold Rome) from *Fanny*—5 lines spoken; 2 lines sung

"I'll Know" (Frank Loesser) from *Guys and Dolls*—17 lines

"Somebody, Somewhere" (Frank Loesser) from *The Most Happy Fella*—5 lines

A few paragraphs earlier I listed some song titles from shows that illustrate the *A A B A* form. It should be noted that some of the songs are different in kind. I will repeat that list here, but this time I will add a *designation* after each title.

"The Man I Love"—ballad

"I Want to Be Happy"—rhythm-ballad, or charm song

"Smoke Gets in Your Eyes"—ballad

"September Song"—ballad

"The Most Beautiful Girl in the World"—charm song

"Wunderbar"—charm song

"Hello, Young Lovers"—ballad

"If Ever I Would Leave You"—ballad

"Just One of Those Things"—charm song

"Bewitched, Bothered and Bewildered"—comedy song

"The Love of My Life"—comedy song

Now let us consider only these designations. They comprise, basically, all of the categories of songs that, together, make up the scores of all shows. Whatever deviations one may occasionally encounter, the songs are nevertheless based on one of these and then sometimes altered in order to accommodate the dramatic needs of the libretto. (These will also be explained later.)

The most common song is the *ballad*. It is important basically as a tune. What the tune has to say specifically is defined by the lyrics, since music itself does not *say* anything. (Remember the form is still *A A B A*.) It is the *character* of the music that categorizes it as a ballad. It may be a love ballad (most frequently) or a narrative or a soliloquy or many other kinds of things; but its principal feature will be its tunefulness, its (usually) *legato*, or smooth, quality. The tunes that one remembers from shows of any kind are usually ballads.

The following is a very brief list of well-known ballads with some indications of their more special categories:

"Will He Like Me?" from *She Loves Me* (music by Jerry Bock, lyrics by Sheldon Harnick)—a love song soliloquy.

"You Don't Remind Me," from *Out of This World* (music and lyrics by Cole Porter)—an oblique love song which says that the object of his affections doesn't remind him of anything but "you."

"Love for Sale," from *The New Yorkers* (music and lyrics by Cole Porter)—the plaint of a prostitute.

"Here in My Arms," from *Dearest Enemy* (music by Richard Rodgers, lyrics by Lorenz Hart)—a tender ballad of frustration.

"Blue Room," from *The Girl Friend* (music by Richard Rodgers, lyrics by Lorenz Hart)—a ballad of happy future plans.

"Ten Cents a Dance," from *Simple Simon* (music by Richard Rodgers, lyrics by Lorenz Hart)—in somewhat the same category as Porter's "Love for Sale," but this one is more tortured.

"There's a Small Hotel," from *On Your Toes* (music by Richard Rodgers, lyrics by Lorenz Hart)—a tender expression of togetherness away from everyone else.

"My Funny Valentine," from *Babes in Arms* (music by Richard Rodgers, lyrics by Lorenz Hart)—akin to "Bill" (see below) in that both songs express affection for someone whose looks are "laughable."

"Bill," from *Show Boat* (music by Jerome Kern, lyrics by P. G. Wodehouse and Oscar Hammerstein II)—similar to above.

"Where or When," from *Babes in Arms* (music by Richard Rogers, lyrics by Lorenz Hart)—remembers love and wonders whether or where or when it occurred.

"Lover, Come Back to Me!" from *The New Moon* (music by Sigmund Romberg, lyrics by Oscar Hammerstein II)—remembers love and laments its absence.

"Ol' Man River," from *Show Boat* (music by Jerome Kern, lyrics by Oscar Hammerstein II)—a non-love ballad; sung by a black man, it contrasts the uninterrupted flow and carelessness of the Mississippi River with his own restricted, unhappy life.

"You Are Love," from *Show Boat* (music by Jerome Kern, lyrics by Oscar Hammerstein II)—a direct love ballad that employs the word "love" without ever resorting to rhyming it. (There are only five words that rhyme with "love": *of, above, shove, glove,* and *dove.*)

"Lonely Room," from *Oklahoma!* (music by Richard Rodgers, lyrics by Oscar Hammerstein II)—not a love ballad, but about love: the singer's comparison of what he would like with the bleakness of his reality.

"If I Loved You," from *Carousel* (music by Richard Rodgers, lyrics by Oscar Hammerstein II)—"flirts" with love through the use of "if," although the meaning in the show is clearly implied—that the singer *does* indeed love.

"Hello, Young Lovers," from *The King and I* (music by Richard Rodgers, lyrics by Oscar Hammerstein II)—addresses all lovers but seeks no pity because her love is dead, since she once had "a love of my own."

"Something Wonderful," from *The King and I* (music by Richard Rodgers, lyrics by Oscar Hammerstein II)—speaks of love felt for someone who can be difficult, and is addressed to someone else whose help she solicits for her beloved.

"Some Enchanted Evening," from *South Pacific* (music by Richard Rodgers, lyrics by Oscar Hammerstein II)—about meeting a love, and it advises "never let her go."

"Younger Than Springtime," from *South Pacific* (music by Richard Rodgers, lyrics by Oscar Hammerstein II)—a direct love song.

"Make Believe," from *Show Boat* (music by Jerome Kern, lyrics by Oscar Hammerstein II)—sung by both boy and girl, a game of pretense in an effort partially to conceal their true feelings (a period piece).

"Someone to Watch Over Me," from *Oh, Kay!* (music by George Gershwin, lyrics by Ira Gershwin)—a girl's plea for love.

"Embraceable You," from *Girl Crazy* (music by George Gershwin, lyrics by Ira Gershwin)—a man wants love.

"Something to Remember You By," from *Three's a Crowd* (music by Arthur Schwartz, lyrics by Howard Dietz)—appeals to a lover who is going away to leave something with him that says "you're my own."

"Dancing in the Dark," from *The Band Wagon* (music by Arthur Schwartz, lyrics by Howard Dietz)—begs for assurance that "we're one."

"If There Is Someone Lovelier Than You," from *Revenge*

With Music (music by Arthur Schwartz, lyrics by Howard Dietz)—answers the song's title: impossible!

"You and the Night and the Music," from *Revenge with Music* (music by Arthur Schwartz, lyrics by Howard Dietz)—begs the question: after dawn, will I still love you?

"April in Paris," from *Walk a Little Faster* (music by Vernon Duke, lyrics by E. Y. Harburg)—states its topic in its title.

"It's Only a Paper Moon," from *The Great Magoo* (music by Vernon Duke, lyrics by E. Y. Harburg)—says that, although everything is "make believe," this would be changed "if you believed in me."

"Over the Rainbow," from *The Wizard of Oz* (film; music by Harold Arlen, lyrics by E. Y. Harburg)—not a love ballad; it yearns for a better world.

"Close as Pages in a Book," from *Up in Central Park* (music by Sigmund Romberg, lyrics by Dorothy Fields)—dreams of how "we'll" be, suggesting that her feeling is only a dream.

"Growing Pains," from *A Tree Grows in Brooklyn* (music by Arthur Schwartz, lyrics by Dorothy Fields)—comments on a young girl's feelings about maturing.

"Make the Man Love Me," from *A Tree Grows in Brooklyn* (music by Arthur Schwartz, lyrics by Dorothy Fields)—a desperate ballad sung by one who is in love with someone whom she is less certain reciprocates her feelings.

"I'll Buy You a Star," from *A Tree Grows in Brooklyn* (music by Arthur Schwartz, lyrics by Dorothy Fields)—promises impossible gifts for his love. It helps enormously to accentuate the fact that the singer is himself a failure, always hoping for better things in the future.

"One of These Fine Days," from *Pins and Needles* (music

and lyrics by Harold Rome)—says that things are going to be better.

"The Red Ball Express," from *Call Me Mister* (music and lyrics by Harold Rome)—a narrative ballad that recalls experiences in World War II.

"The Face on the Dime," from *Call Me Mister* (music and lyrics by Harold Rome)—extols F.D.R. and mourns his passing.

"Welcome Home," from *Fanny* (music and lyrics by Harold Rome)—expresses joy at returning home.

"I Like You," from *Fanny* (music and lyrics by Harold Rome)—a boy's awkward attempt to tell his father that he loves him.

"To My Wife," from *Fanny* (music and lyrics by Harold Rome)—a song of gratitude that expresses love without passion.

"Love Is a Very Light Thing," from *Fanny* (music and lyrics by Harold Rome)—a ballad of wonderment at the composition of a new baby.

"I'll Know," from *Guys and Dolls* (music and lyrics by Frank Loesser)—a bitter duet in which the tight-laced girl imagines what her love will be like and the man taunts her for her prudery.

"I've Never Been in Love Before," from *Guys and Dolls* (music and lyrics by Frank Loesser)—expresses love by saying that he/she never before experienced it.

"Somebody, Somewhere," from *The Most Happy Fella* (music and lyrics by Frank Loesser)—an impassioned ballad sung by a girl who is thrilled by someone's wanting and needing her.

"Joey, Joey, Joey," from *The Most Happy Fella* (music and lyrics by Frank Loesser)—a non-love song about wanderlust and the incessant lure of the unknown.

"I Believe in You," from *How to Succeed in Business Without*

Really Trying (music and lyrics by Frank Loesser)—in the show it's a comedy song, since the hero sings it to and about himself. Separated from the show, it becomes a love ballad to another person.

"Lonely Town," from *On the Town* (music by Leonard Bernstein, lyrics by Betty Comden and Adolph Green) —expresses the pain of singleness in a city.

"Lucky to Be Me," from *On the Town* (music by Leonard Bernstein, lyrics by Betty Comden and Adolph Green) —exults in the joy of having found love.

"Some Other Time," from *On the Town* (music by Leonard Bernstein, lyrics by Betty Comden and Adolph Green)—expresses the sadness of parting.

"Long Before I Knew You," from *Bells Are Ringing* (music by Jule Styne, lyrics by Betty Comden and Adolph Green)—says, in conclusion, that he loved her before he knew her.

"The Party's Over," from *Bells Are Ringing* (music by Jule Styne, lyrics by Betty Comden and Adolph Green)— laments the end of a dream of love.

"Camelot," from *Camelot* (music by Frederick Loewe, lyrics by Alan Jay Lerner)—an apostrophe to a place.

"If Ever I Would Leave You," from *Camelot* (music by Frederick Loewe, lyrics by Alan Jay Lerner)—says that the lover can never leave his love at any time.

"There But for You Go I," from *Brigadoon* (music by Frederick Loewe, lyrics by Alan Jay Lerner)—expresses gratitude for "you" who have kept "me" from being lonely.

"From This Day On," from *Brigadoon* (music by Frederick Lowe, lyrics by Alan Jay Lerner)—sung at a time of parting, it says that the singer will always love only her/him.

"I've Grown Accustomed to Her Face," from *My Fair*

Lady (music by Frederick Loewe, lyrics by Alan Jay Lerner)—a ballad of unhappiness at missing someone who is absent.

"Do You Love Me?" from *Fiddler on the Roof* (music by Jerry Bock, lyrics by Sheldon Harnick)—a comic and touching dialogue between a husband and wife of twenty-five years. The wife is stunned by her husband's outrageous question, one that had never occurred to either of them before.

"Go to Sleep, Whatever You Are," from *The Apple Tree* (music by Jerry Bock, lyrics by Sheldon Harnick)—a kind of lullaby sung by Eve to her firstborn child. She is tender but puzzled.

"Far From the Home I Love," from *Fiddler on the Roof* (music by Jerry Bock, lyrics by Sheldon Harnick)—a ballad of parting.

"Send in the Clowns," from *A Little Night Music* (music and lyrics by Stephen Sondheim)—a "philosophical" ballad.

Of course, there are many others—models of ballad-writing in a variety of other ways. This rather lengthy list will, however, serve the present purposes amply.

Now, there is no sharp difference between some ballads and some "charm songs," our next consideration. *Charm songs* are, in my definition, songs with steady rhythmic accompaniments and an optimistic feeling (optimistic lyrics), with a steadier sense of movement than one finds in most ballads.

The following is a list of songs in this category. In several instances, I have applied both appelations to a single song:

"Whistle a Happy Tune," from *The King and I* (Rodgers and Hammerstein)

"Mountain Greenery," from *Garrick Gaities* (Rodgers and Hart)

"Bidin' My Time," from *Girl Crazy* (George and Ira Gershwin)

"I Got Plenty o' Nuttin'," from *Porgy and Bess* (George and Ira Gershwin)

"The Surrey with the Fringe on Top," from *Oklahoma!* (Rodgers and Hammerstein)

"It's a Grand Night for Singing," from *State Fair* (film; Rodgers and Hammerstein)

"Luck Be a Lady Tonight," from *Guys and Dolls* (Frank Loesser)

"Once in Love with Amy," from *Where's Charley?* (Frank Loesser)

"Fine and Dandy," from *Fine and Dandy* (Paul James and Kay Swift)

"I Guess I'll Have to Change My Plans," from *The Little Show* (Arthur Schwartz and Howard Dietz)

"I Feel Pretty," from *West Side Story* (Leonard Bernstein and Stephen Sondheim)

"My Heart Belongs to Daddy," from *Leave It to Me* (Cole Porter)

"Manhattan," from *Garrick Gaities* (Richard Rodgers and Lorenz Hart)—could also be considered a comedy song, chiefly because of the amusing use of rhyme.

"Johnny One Note," from *Babes in Arms* (Richard Rodgers and Lorenz Hart)

"I Got Rhythm," from *Girl Crazy* (George and Ira Gershwin)

"I Love Louisa," from *The Band Wagon* (Arthur Schwartz and Howard Dietz)

"I Feel a Song Coming On," from *Every Night at Eight* (film; Jimmy McHugh and Dorothy Fields)

"Love Is the Reason," from *A Tree Grows in Brooklyn* (Arthur Schwartz and Dorothy Fields)

"Be Kind to Your Parents," from *Fanny* (Harold Rome)

14

"Standing on the Corner," from *The Most Happy Fella* (Frank Loesser)

"Just in Time," from *Bells Are Ringing* (Jule Styne, and Betty Comden and Adolph Green)

and many others.

The optimistic or genial or happy character of *charm songs,* in some instances, crossbreeds them with *comedy songs.* The music of charm songs is often as equally important as the lyrics, but in my opinion no *comedy song* is worthy of that name unless the lyrics—the all-important factor—are funny. The music *may* have importance, but it usually serves as a kind of accompaniment to the words. Music by itself cannot be funny, and the song is funny only if the words make it so. Successful comedy songs are the most difficult to come by, and I will reserve a discussion of their creation for the section dealing with lyrics.

Fourth and last in the list of basic theatre songs is the *musical scene,* in which music, lyrics, dramatic situation, and dialogue may be of equal importance. The form is widely variable and may serve one of a number of purposes. Here, for a better understanding of what a musical scene may be, I will resort briefly to history.

We are familiar with musical theatre lineage—that it began with opera, took on a lighter side with operetta and similar forms bearing other titles in other countries. In opera, I would call the famous quartet from *Rigoletto,* Leporello's aria "Madamina, il Catalogo è questo" in *Don Giovanni,* the Card Scene in Carmen (a trio), and "Un Bel Di" from *Madama Butterfly* all musical scenes. Also, the finale of Act I in any operetta by Gilbert and Sullivan, and the Act I finale of *Rose Marie.* Now, what do such diverse musical numbers have in common?

Some involve one character; one, three; one, four; and the

finales referred to involve an entire cast and ensemble. Each of them is *larger*—in form—than just a song. Each has a dramatic beginning, development, and conclusion: all of them *progress.*

Rose Marie (1924)—The Act I finale contains songs, dramatic recitatives, spoken dialogue, and reprises. The thematic material used as background music employs the title song ("Rose Marie"), "Lak' Jeem," "The Mounties," and "Indian Theme" (some of these several times); then vocal reprises (or partial ones) of "Lak' Jeem," "The Mounties," "Hard-Boiled Herman," "Indian Love Call" are used to illustrate plot points, and these musical scenes also employ vocally almost the entire company. There is also, occasionally, spoken dialogue over continuing music.

The Student Prince (1924)—The Act I finale also contains songs, dramatic recitatives, spoken dialogue, and reprises. Background music includes themes from "Golden Days," and reprises include "Drinking Song," but, unlike *Rose Marie,* there is also new material of importance, such as "Serenade" and "When the Spring."

The Desert Song (1926)—The Act I finale employs all materials as in the above operettas. In addition, it contains a dance for dramatic (plot) purposes, and introduces an important new song, "Soft as a Pigeon Lights Upon the Sand." It finishes with a reprise of the title song.

The Mikado (1885)—The Act I finale serves to introduce an important character (Katisha); it has no reprises, but contains all the elements of speech, solo song, and ensemble singing generally used for pseudo-dramatic purposes ("pseudo" only because it intends to lampoon serious operatic practices). In *The Mikado* Act I finale, there is nothing but *new* musical material.

The Vagabond King (1925)—The Act I finale begins orchestrally with "Song of the Vagabonds." Then there is dramatic dialogue set to music (recitative), after which we return to underscoring made from the "Song of the Vagabonds," then to a large ensemble-plus-principals *arrangement* of "Someday." These illustrations are from the past. In my own opinion, because of this very fact, American composers and writers for the musical theatre began to regard the *musical scene* as an old-fashioned melodramatic device. In the examples I have just cited, all but the one from *Don Giovanni* are melodramatic. Hence the musical scene fell into disrepute and was absent from new musical shows from about 1926 until about 1940, although Jerome Kern, who was a conscious prober into the materials of musicals, did employ it in *Show Boat* and later, more lightly (I refer to the mood) than ever before, in the musical play *The Cat and the Fiddle.* Here the musical scene was used for charm in dramatic sequences that were larger and looser in form than songs.

Still later, the device has been used by all present-day or recent writers, sometimes melodramatically, sometimes dramatically, for charm and for comedy. Examples follow:

"Happy to Make Your Acquaintance," from *The Most Happy Fella* (Frank Loesser)—charm, involving three characters

"A Boy Like That"—"I Have a Love," from *West Side Story* (Stephen Sondheim and Leonard Bernstein)—dramatic development

"Shall We Dance," from *The King and I* (Rodgers and Hammerstein)—charm, ending abruptly with drama

"The Rain in Spain," from *My Fair Lady* (Lerner and Loewe)—charm

"I've Grown Accustomed to Her Face," from *My Fair Lady* (Lerner and Loewe)—regret and anger

"A Hymn to Him," ("Why Can't a Woman Be More Like a Man?") from *My Fair Lady* (Lerner and Loewe)—comedy

"Eat a Little Something," from *I Can Get It for You Whole-sale* (Harold Rome)—bitterness

"Anything You Can Do I Can Do Better," from *Annie Get Your Gun* (Irving Berlin)—comedy

"Sue Me," from *Guys and Dolls* (Frank Loesser)—comedy

"Glitter and Be Gay," from *Candide* (Richard Wilbur and Leonard Bernstein)—satire

"You Must Meet My Wife," from *A Little Night Music* (Stephen Sondheim)—comedy

"Rose's Turn," from *Gypsy* (Stephen Sondheim and Jule Styne)—dramatic situation

The different uses of music and lyrics in a musical have now been defined and illustrated. Later, I will describe assignments which I urge interested composers and lyricists to try their hands at, not once, but several times.

THE MUSICAL ELEMENTS

Meanwhile, let us consider the musical elements which are employed in the creation of all of these songs. They are:

melody

harmony

rhythm

form (previously described)

All these elements, but the first three in particular, are inter-dependent. Briefly, harmony, unless it is artificially superim-posed, as in too many overfancy "arrangements," is inherent in melody.

In the following examples, I will first present a melody, then indicate its *inherent* harmony. Likewise, rhythm is inherent in the melody which it should *serve*, and to a smaller extent the harmonies also control or are controlled by the rhythm. The "rightness" of either way (there are no rules) is dependent upon the specific case.

"IN JANUARY LAST" (*circa* 1679)

This harmonization is simple and seems to have been dictated by the melody and the style. When I said previously that the rhythm also contributes to some extent to the method of harmonization, I would point here to the first three melodic notes, all of which belong to the tonic chord of E major (the key of the song). However, because the first note is a "pick-up" and occurs prior to the bar-line, to include this in the same harmony (I) would be to deprive the song of an initial impetus: therefore, the first note is harmonized as IV.

But melody, which has so much importance in the theatre —regardless of its style—should be as rememberable as possible. A good one consists of two major ingredients: repetition; and "travel," or movement.

The following—the famous waltz from *The Merry Widow* by Franz Lehar—will illustrate both.

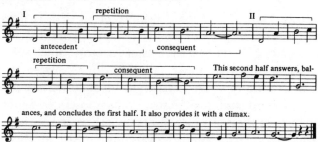

"Travel" in this case is not in itself motion but occurs because the tune breaks out of the mold established by the two repetitions in the first four bars.

Because the original interval between the first two notes is a fourth, and in II is a fifth, this second series is already a kind of development. Note also that the fifth bar begins a tone higher than anything in bars one through four. The same thing happens in the fifth bar of II. The second section (beginning at bar seventeen) reaches the biggest melodic climax. The first four bars of section two are "repeated" in the next four, a third lower. The final eight bars constitute a summation windup, or ending for the entire theme.

"Travel," in all uses in connection with melody, means moving *away from,* not necessarily just moving.

There is a harmonic idea which is not not often clearly comprehended. For example, there is a pronounced tendency to return too frequently to the original or tonic key. This is preceded by the dominant harmony, which easily allows for this obvious resolution. What one encounters less often, and is most valuable and more difficult to effect, is a kind of "harmonic suspensiveness." This is accomplished by creation of an all-important sense of (harmonic) tension that generates a feeling of "pushing ahead" as opposed to "settling down" or resolution. Ideally, most resolutions should occur only at the finish of a song. One may and usually does occur at the end of the first A section.

Rhythm should be employed more often than is usual to provide a sense of propulsion to the music. Even ballads too frequently bog down in a morass of lethargy, since this idea of sentiment (mostly romantic) is felt to be violated by any intrusion of energy. This lethargic breakdown is contrary even to the songs of such romantic composers as Schubert, Schumann, Brahms, Strauss and many others in whose works the accompaniments almost invariably consist of rhythmic figures that—combined with progressing harmonies—provide an invaluable feeling of movement.

If the composers of rock songs in the Sixties accomplished nothing else (and in the opinion of this writer, there was indeed litle else), they did reenforce the feeling of rhythmic propulsion. Unfortunately, this most often was based on only a single "non-pattern": the repetition of a chord—too often the *same* chord—and invariably on every beat of the song.

The classical (romantic) song composers mentioned above employed a wide variety of accompaniments that were rhythmically propulsive and harmonically suspensive, and it would be wise for today's songwriter to study these.

There is, of course, no formula for creating anything, but these *principles* are to be found in all music, regardless of style or period. While the degree of rememberableness will depend on many ephemeral things, the *crafting* of a melody can be learned. Its ultimate success depends first on talent, then on knowing what to do with it, and then finally on the degree of exposure given the melody—a subject to be discussed separately.

This rememberableness of a song—if indeed it is intrinsically *worth* remembering—is related (as I have already said) to repetition of the song as an entity, also to its resemblance to older-style songs in general, as well as to some song in particular. This last can, in some instances, barely skirt plagiarism. Sometimes the similarity is just enough to make the "newer" song much easier to recall than a wholly fresh one. Oftentimes, the newer song, while not specifically like any other, belongs so definitely to an older, well-established style that it might have been written half a century earlier by the composer who founded that already well-explored dynasty.

But repetition is a helpful factor that can lead to remembering and even (finally) to comprehension. All of us have experienced this, even with the symphonies of Beethoven, now more than one and a half centuries old. We have experienced it with much newer works, such as *The Rite of Spring* by Stravinsky. Familiarity at first yields guideposts that we begin to anticipate and, on encountering again, welcome as old friends.

Contrast is of enormous importance in all manifestations of opera, operetta, musical comedy, symphony, and the rest. The most obvious contrast is employed in the symphony, which, classically, was in four movements. Here you find the first briskly moving, the second usually slow and lyrical, the third often a playful scherzo, and the last a fast, serious piece.

A musical artist building a concert program contrasts moods, speeds (tempi), and keys (tonalities). Just so, the composer of a musical show must construct it with care so that songs of similar mood and tempo do not, if at all possible, follow one another. Let us take out the songs in four representative musical shows, place them outside the connecting dialogue, list them as they appear in the show, and categorize them:

Naughty Marietta (1910)—VICTOR HERBERT and
RIDA JOHNSON YOUNG

ACT I

Bright chorus
Marching song
Light chorus
Charm song (solo)
Charm song (duet)
Bright duet
Ballad
Fast aria ("Italian Street Song")
Fast-changing dramatic finale

ACT II

Charm duet
Fast ballad
Scherzo dance
Intermezzo ("Ah! Sweet Mystery of Life")
Fast chorus

Song-and-dance pastiche
Ballad
Waltz song
Ballad ("I'm Falling in Love with Someone")
Comedy song
Ballad ("Ah! Sweet Mystery of Life")

It is also important to observe the contrast in the characters (or ensembles) who sing the songs, and the number of songs given to the principal performers. The characters are noted after each song.

Annie Get Your Gun (1946)—IRVING BERLIN

ACT I

Musical scene (march), Charlie (secondary) and ensemble
Charm song and dance, Frank (hero)
Comedy song ("Doin' What Comes Natur'lly"), Annie (heroine), children, and Wilson (small part)
Ballad ("The Girl That I Marry"), Frank (hero)
Fast charm song ("You Can't Get a Man with a Gun"), Annie (heroine)
Rhythm song ("Show Business"), Charlie, Buffalo Bill, Frank, and Annie
Ballad duet ("They Say It's Wonderful"), Frank and Annie
Charm song ("Moonshine Lullaby"), Annie and male ensemble
Comedy song (duet and dance), Tommy and Winnie (secondary)
Dance
Reprise ("Show Business") instrumental
Circus Dance
Reprise ("Show Business"), Annie

Rhythm Song ("My Defenses Are Down"), Frank and
male ensemble
Production number (dance and chant)
Rhythm song ("I'm an Indian"), Annie
Finale (Background: "The Girl That I Marry" and "You
Can't Get a Man"), Annie

ACT II

Ballad ("I Got Lost in His Arms"), Annie and mixed
ensemble
Charm duet and dance ("Who Do You Love, I Hope"),
Tommy and Winnie
"Jump" song ("I Got the Sun in the Morning"), Annie
and mixed ensemble
Ballad reprise ("They Say It's Wonderful"), Annie and
Frank
Ballad reprise ("The Girl That I Marry"), Frank
Comedy song ("Anything You Can Do"), Annie and
Frank
Finale ("Show Business" and "They Say It's Wonderful"),
ensemble

South Pacific (1947)—RICHARD RODGERS and
OSCAR HAMMERSTEIN II, with JOSHUA LOGAN

ACT I

Charm song ("Dites-Moi"), two children
Charm song ("A Cockeyed Optimist"), Nellie (hero-
ine)
"Twin Soliloquies"—Nellie and Emile (hero)
Ballad ("Some Enchanted Evening"), Emile
Reprise ("Some Enchanted Evening"), Emile
Finaletto ("Dites-Moi"), two children
Rhythm song ("Bloody Mary"), male chorus

Rhythm song ("There Is Nothing Like a Dame"), male chorus

Ballad ("Bali Ha'i"), Bloody Mary (secondary character)

Reprise ("Bali Ha'i"), Lt. Cable (subplot romantic lead)

Charm song ("I'm Gonna Wash That Man Right Outa My Hair"), Nellie and female ensemble

Reprise ("Some Enchanted Evening"), Emile and Nellie

Charm song ("I'm in Love with a Wonderful Guy"), Nellie

Reprise ("Bali Ha'i"), female ensemble

Ballad ("Younger Than Springtime"), Lt. Cable and Liat (young lovers)

Reprise ("I'm in Love with a Wonderful Guy"), Nellie and Emile

Charm song ("This Is How It Feels"), Nellie and Emile

Reprise ("I'm Gonna Wash That Man"), Emile

Finale Act I ("Some Enchanted Evening"), Emile

ACT II

Charm song ("Happy Talk"), Bloody Mary

Charm song ("Honey Bun"), Nellie and male ensemble with Billis

Ballad ("Carefully Taught"), Lt. Cable

Ballad ("This Nearly Was Mine"), Emile

Much incidental music with partial reprises

Finale ("Dites-Moi"), Nellie, Emile, and children

Summary of Character Song Assignments

In *Annie Get Your Gun*

Annie (solos, duets, etc.)	12 songs
Frank	8 songs
Tommy and Winnie	2 songs and dances
Charles	2 songs

25

In *South Pacific*

Nellie	9 songs
Emile	9 songs
Bloody Mary	2 songs
Lt. Cable	3 songs
Liat	1 song
Billis	1 song

MUSICAL LAYOUT

Next we must consider the "layout" of a song. Although this will require some elucidation, the possibilities of its use and combinations of use will instantly appear limitless.

To begin with, a composer writes a song: a verse and a chorus. Perhaps the lyricist will provide several sets of lyrics, indicating the possibility of repetition. (In a narrative song, repetition is mandatory.) With or without different lyrics, this verse-followed-by-chorus is the basic song before it has been set in its particular niche in the show. The following will indicate a few of the many possible "layouts":

"Some Enchanted Evening," from *South Pacific*—chorus (with short coda).

"Hello, Young Lovers," from *The King and I*—verse, chorus.

"I'll Know," from *Guys and Dolls*—verse I, chorus I, verse II, chorus II.

"Make Believe," from *Show Boat*—chorus I, interlude (which is in three parts), chorus II.

"They Say It's Wonderful," from *Annie Get Your Gun*—chorus I, verse, chorus II (incomplete) played under dialogue, last six bars sung.

"To My Wife," from *Fanny*—chorus, six bars of chorus under dialogue, last four bars sung.

"Wunderbar," from *Kiss Me, Kate*—last sixteen bars of

chorus under dialogue, same sixteen bars as vocal, verse, chorus II sung completely, release *(B)* as dance, last sixteen bars *(A)* sung.

"The Surrey with the Fringe on Top," from *Oklahoma!*— verse I, chorus I, verse II, chorus II, verse III played under dialogue, chorus III sung.

These layouts are dependent upon:

1. the worth of the song;
2. its tempo (fast or slow);
3. the importance of the singing character to the show;
4. the *type* of lyrics.

Each of these conditions requires explanation:

1. Worth is fairly obvious. If the song seems stage-worthy, musically interesting, singable, and likeable, a general desire on the part of many of the collaborators to hear it again will make repetition mandatory. Examples: "The Surrey with the Fringe on Top," from *Oklahoma!;* "There's No Business Like Show Business," from *Annie Get Your Gun.*

2. A fast song is more frequently repeated than a slow song, if only because a second or third repetition will consume less time than a slow one, and will *seem* less tedious to the audience.

3. If the singer of the song is a principal character in the show or a star (in or out of the show), the song she (he) sings will appear more attractive. Consequently, a repetition of the song will be more welcome than if it is sung by a nonentity.

"More I Cannot Wish You," from *Guys and Dolls,* is a charming song, but it is slow and sung only once by a secondary character.

4. The lyrics may be narrative, that is, they may tell a tale that, for completion, may require many choruses. Examples: "Saga of Jenny," from *Lady in the Dark;* "The Surrey with the Fringe on Top," from *Oklahoma!;* "The Miller's Son," from *A*

Little Night Music; "Nothing," from *A Chorus Line;* "True Love," from *St. Louis Woman;* "Chrysanthemum Tea," from *Pacific Overtures;* and "Where is the Tribe for Me?" from *Bajour.* Notice that in all of these songs, the lyrics *require* musical repetition for the unfolding of their narrative, and *the music is not slow.*

All these (and many other) possibilities of repetition through the layout of a song may occur in a single spot in the unfolding of a show. In addition, there is the *reprise,* the repetition of a song in another part of the show, sung again by the same character or by one or more different characters.

In the early American operetta-type musicals, these reprises were employed less frequently than one would imagine. In their Viennese precursors, they were used even less often. Examples: "Play Gypsies! Dance Gypsies!" from *Countess Maritza* (twice); "Sigismund," from *The White Horse Inn* (three times); "I Want to Be Happy," from *No, No Nanette* (twice).

In the musical comedies of the Twenties, they were more often heard again in first- or second-act finales. In the big shows of the Forties, Fifties, Sixties, and Seventies, reprises were employed with increasing frequency. Examples: "Only a Rose" (three times), "Some Day" (twice), and "Song of the Vagabonds" (seven times), from *The Vagabond King;* "Lover, Come Back to Me," from *The New Moon* (twice); "Drinking Song" (twice), "Golden Days" (three times), Serenade (twice), and "Deep in My Heart" (twice), from *The Student Prince;* "The Girl That I Marry" (four times), "You Can't Get a Man With a Gun" (five times), "Show Business" (eight times), "They Say It's Wonderful" (six times), from *Annie Get Your Gun;* five part-reprises are used together for dramatic purpose in *Brigadoon.*

Today, in Stephen Sondheim's *A Little Night Music*, "Send in the Clowns" is reprised only in part near the end of the show, and is employed for dramatic reasons. The only other repetition is "Weekend in the Country," repeated several times, at the close of Act I.

There is one incontrovertible fact: repetitions within the song's form, repetitions in its layout, and reprises on various levels did indeed din certain songs into the consciousness of audiences. Today, with the almost negligible use of reprise, there is less remembering.

Besides—and this is the final point—the evolution of scenic art has had a large effect on this dinning process. At the time of, say, *Annie Get Your Gun* (1946), there were frequent scene shiftings. Each time, for eight bars (or as many bars as the shift required—it varied somewhat nightly), the orchestra played scene-change music. Much of this was song-repetition. Today, with most scenery changed in view of the audience, or with the employment of unit sets, scene-change music has been abandoned, and this once-useful musical repetition has generally been discarded. Overtures—often not listened to by audiences—containing many of the show's principal tunes, have largely been abandoned. Making overtures is expensive, and since they have been generally disregarded, producers have felt no need to use them. In *Candide*, Bernstein *composed* an overture—an almost unique happening that made a special event out of the piece. Without the overture as an "introducer" of tunes, they are heard even less frequently. Tunes definitely exist today, but their infrequent repetition makes them *seem* unimportant.

The Lyrics

ALTHOUGH MUSIC CAN do many things, one of the things it cannot do is impart a *specific* idea. In the most general sense it can connote pleasure, suggest sensuality, be impish, sad, martial, funereal, triumphant, and can impart other general qualities. It cannot, in the theatre, pinpoint a character, be *specific* about the emotions of love, hate, fear. It cannot tell a story, create laughter or tears. (I can hear the reader who has read romantic tales about Tchaikovsky's *Pathétique* Symphony say that it has made him weep. However, without the tales and without the title—a word that in itself suggests a tale, I am certain that the music alone would not cause tears.)

The lyric is the element that, combined with the music, can define the singer of the song, tell us exactly where it is that we are going, what we are thinking and feeling. It is, therefore, the obligation of the lyricist to say precisely what he means to say, to find images and rhymes that are fresh and not dull with overusage, that—unlike most non-theatre lyrics—*go* somewhere.

The lyricists should always remember that, unlike poetry, lyrics for a song are intended *only* to be heard: they are addressed to the ear. Moreover, they are heard together with the music, a fact which can create some complications, although when lyrics are simple and clear and music provides the proper complement to them, they should reach the listener's ears and mind meaningfully. However, any *question* as to the precise meaning of the words is likely to cause the listener to pause, to consider, to "turn off" what immediately follows in order to try to unravel whatever it is that has puzzled him.

These "puzzlements" may be caused by any of several different things. The words may simply not say clearly what the writer has in mind or what he *thinks* he has said. Or he may have used one of the many sound-alike words in our language that nevertheless have unrelated meanings. ("Too" [i.e., "also"]) may be employed in such a way that the hearer may ponder the possibility that the word is actually "two.") Or the construction of the sentence, together with the rhythmic setting of the music (musical pauses that blur the meaning) may tend to obscure the lyricist's intention. ("To be all—that you want/Can be more than—a dream.") The lyricist should examine his writing honestly and carefully for any possible ambivalence before releasing it to his composer (if they work in the manner of lyrics first, then music), and then reexamine it after it has been set to music to be certain that it *sounds* as clear as he had intended after he has heard it attached to or integrated with the music.

The lyric of a theatre song should be complete and should contain the character information necessary to define the particular person singing the song. A single central idea (topic) should be expressed, and, like a three-act play, it should have a setup, development, and *resolution*.

Now there is one aspect of this character self-revelation that is not often discussed, but I feel it is an important consideration in theatre lyric-writing. We are well aware that the words of a song are built on the development of a topic. For example, the topic of Oscar Hammerstein's "Something Wonderful" in *The King and I* has to do with the peculiar though admirable qualities of the king. The singer of the song is Lady Thiang, the king's favorite wife and mother of his heir to the throne. Prior to the song there has been a serious argument between the unreasonable king and Mrs. Anna, the imported Welsh teacher of the king's many children and wives. Mrs. Anna has already been of great help to the king, but she has left him *angrily* and is in her own living quarters in the palace, refusing to see him. Lady Thiang has come to call on Mrs. Anna and, through this song, tries to demonstrate the king's "wonderful" qualities, all the while incorporating in these a recognition of his faults: she is trying to persuade Mrs. Anna to return to the king who needs her. This is the *function* of the song, and the king is the *topic*.

However, something else of infinite importance emerges, perhaps like the aroma of good cooking: the *purpose* in cooking is the preparation of food, the *topic* is the food itself (roast beef, curried lamb, baked fish, etc.). Nevertheless, the aroma is experienced and adds immeasurably to the enjoyment of the dish.

Just so, in addition to the purpose of "Something Wonderful" and the topic of its lyrics, the important "aroma" that permeates the song is the *character* of Lady Thiang, who sings it. She is recognized as kind, warm, devoted, self-effacing, and —simple as she is—as attempting to reconcile the two warring factions, both far stronger and more important than she.

To cite two other examples (and in the best shows there are

countless others), Sister Sarah, in Frank Loesser's *Guys and Dolls*, sings "I'll Know" (when my love comes along). She describes in the song the kind of man she will accept as her ideal love, but the song more importantly reveals Sister Sarah's maddening inexperience and narrowmindedness.

In *Company*, Stephen Sondheim wrote "The Ladies Who Lunch" for one of the principal female characters. The song's topic is defined by the title, and it is this topic that is developed throughout. However, while the song entertains, it also says through the singer's point of view what she herself is really like: sophisticated, abrasive, frustrated, and bitter about life.

It is important to note that in none of these songs does the character verbalize any of the self-facts. They emerge only *above* what she has to say about something or somebody else.

Here are some other lyrics that delineate character:

"Lonely Room," from *Oklahoma!*
"Hello, Young Lovers," from *The King and I*
"Soliloquy," from *Carousel*
"If I Were a Rich Man," from *Fiddler on the Roof*
"I'm an Ordinary Man," from *My Fair Lady*
"My Time of Day," from *Guys and Dolls*
"Adelaide's Lament," from *Guys and Dolls*
"Joey, Joey, Joey," from *The Most Happy Fella*

Unquestionably, love songs (usually ballads) are the most common of all types of songs in musical shows. For a long time now, they have become clichés because too many writers of books and lyrics have made them predictable and have settled too easily for, in essence, "I Love You." We have not only heard this too often for it to remain effective, but with the changing mores these words have become almost meaningless. Unless the spectator is made to believe thoroughly in the credibility, honesty, and perhaps naïveté of the characters, these words at most are only ritualistic. Once, when they were meaningful, they pointed to a forever future. Today they most frequently indicate an impassioned, immediate sexual desire.

In most musical shows of the past, finding two attractive young people—boy and girl—on stage together was the automatic cue to composer and lyricist to provide a love song. The two young people seemed unquestionably "right" for one another, the audience was made to want them together, and only outside interference or misunderstanding could conceivably part them long enough to keep the show's curtain aloft for better than two hours.

Examples of such songs and their motivations follow, although these examples are by no means exhaustive.

In *Good News* (1927), by DeSylva, Schwab, Brown, and Henderson, there are two boy-girl songs, and both, surprisingly, are in Act I. There is a reprise of one in Act II. The first, "The Best Things in Life Are Free," emerges out of the girl's saying that she is "sort of a poor relation." The boy indicates that it doesn't matter, then asks: "You have a boyfriend, haven't you?" The girl gives a negative reply and the boy answers, just before the song, "You have, too!"

The song itself was a great hit, and even after half a century, both lyrics and music and the very *idea* seem fresh. What has tarnished most severely is the coy way in which it is introduced in the show.

The other boy-girl song in the same act is "Lucky in Love." Again, the boy skittishly says he's not a betting man but he'd bet that *this* love would last forever if *she* wanted it to. The song itself reiterates the boy's unluckiness in gambling, but on the other hand if the girl will have him, he'll be lucky in love —bright, light, predictable, and mindless.

In *The New Moon* (1935), Hammerstein, Mandel, Schwab, Romberg, and his collaborators tried to do something fairly new. The hero—very early in the show—sings a song, an apostrophe to his love, Marianne: "Marianne, I want to love you. . . ." Shortly afterward, it is repeated by his sailors, then carried on by Marianne herself. When the two—Robert and Marianne—are together later in the act and sing "Wanting You"—one of the best-remembered songs in the show—the lyrics are for the most part what we would expect.

Early in Act I of *The Three Musketeers* (1927) by McGuire, Wodehouse, Grey, and Romberg, D'Artagnon meets his Constance and they sing a duet, "Heart of Mine," which, in effect, says "all my life I've been looking for you."

In *The Desert Song*, when the Red Shadow is alone with the heroine, Margot, for the first time, he sings "Blue Heaven" (sometimes called "The Desert Song"), the sole point of which is "I love you."

In *Pal Joey* (1940), Vera Simpson, the wealthy older heroine, sings "Bewitched, Bothered and Bewildered," which *tells* of her infatuation, but it is not a love song. Later in the show, Vera and Joey have a duet, "Den of Iniquity," in which the sophisticated Vera actually makes fun of her life with Joey, and Joey stupidly concurs, not realizing that Vera is being flip. In *Oklahoma!* (1943), the hero and heroine sing more obliquely of their love in "People Will Say We're in Love." In *Carousel* (1945), the hero and heroine sing "If I Lov*ed* You"! In *The Pajama Game* (1954) by Adler, Ross, Abbott, and Bissell, in Scene 3 when the heroine sings to a group "I'm not at all in love . . . ," the meaning is clearly the reverse of the words, and the lady does not sing the song in the presence of, or to, the hero.

We are moving nearer the present time, when it seems obvious that the best lyricists are concerned with both newer ways of saying "I love you" and eschewing attempts at saying it every time the hero and heroine are alone together.

The difficult problems which have been resolved many times are: (1) finding and using fresh lyrical images; and (2) selecting situations that are not obvious for saying it. The following are some detailed and recommended examples of love songs that are not lyrically stereotyped, and that also emerge out of nonstereotyped situations.

First, in *Carousel* (1945) by Rodgers and Hammerstein, the song occurs early in the show. The boy-girl have seen each other during the pantomimed first scene, and have met and are becoming acquainted in Scene 2. Each is attracted to the other. The girl has decided that she loves the boy, but has never said that she does. The boy is physically strong but he is defensive about love. The song is sung first by the girl, then a short while later is repeated by the boy. The clue to the difference between this and other earlier love songs is to be found in the title "If I Loved You." The girl sings it to put the boy at ease, to tell him that she doesn't love him—an untruth. The boy sings it after saying that he doesn't love her but that "it'd be awful" if he did.

In *My Fair Lady* (1956) by Alan Jay Lerner and Frederick Loewe, no love song is ever sung by either of the principals. However, the situation at the start of the final scene is the result of the heroine's having left the stuffy hero (who has taught her to speak correctly) because he was unable to treat her like a human being. Neither, at least verbally, has ever considered the other romantically. The hero is lonely. He sings "I've Grown Accustomed to Her Face"—at first a song of sentimental reminiscence. At regular intervals he becomes violently irritated at the thought of her. These vituperative soliloquies alternate between moments of tender recollection. She returns, now understanding him. When the final curtain descends, the music of "I've Grown Accustomed to Her Face" swells and the heroine advances toward the hero. Whatever romance there actually is, is supplied, wishfully, by the audience.

In Stephen Sondheim's *A Funny Thing Happened on the Way to the Forum* (1962), young love is represented by Hero, an attractive young man, and Philia, "a virgin" who lives next door in a whorehouse. The song is called "Lovely" and is sung by the two young people early in Act I. It has been clearly established before the song that Hero is smitten with Philia and that the latter, though attractive, is stupid. This is an original idea. The amusing lyrics add to the freshness and humor. Their culmination and end are (loveliness) ". . . a gift for me to share with you!" No effort is made to upgrade Philia's dumbness. Although she is, in fact, the young heroine, she has nothing but physical beauty. This is a love song that makes us laugh at other love songs.

The final analyzed example of "considered" love songs is from Act II of *Fiddler on the Roof* (1964) by Sheldon Harnick and Jerry Bock. This one is truly unexpected, for several reasons. Called "Do You Love Me?" it is really a "musical scene" (larger than a song) that gets its impetus from the middle-aged hero's question to his unromantic, industrious wife of twenty-five years, "Do you love me?" It comes as a surprise to her since they had never before considered the question, although they had brought up five daughters and lived and worked together during twenty-five years without once having thought of anything beyond the fact that they were married. This song for two plain, middle-aged people, mated originally by tradition, comes as a delightful miracle.

The following is a list of other freshly conceived theatrical love songs:

"You Don't Remind Me," from *Out of This World* (Porter)
"Manhattan," from *Garrick Gaities* (Rodgers and Hart)
"Bill," from *Show Boat* (Wodehouse, Hammerstein, and Kern)
"There's a Small Hotel," from *On Your Toes* (Rodgers and Hart)

"My Funny Valentine," from *Babes in Arms* (Rodgers and Hart)

"They Were You," from *The Fantasticks* (Schmidt and Jones)

"Lucky to Be Me," from *On the Town* (Comden and Green, and Bernstein)

"I'll Buy You a Star," from *A Tree Grows in Brooklyn* (Fields and Schwartz)

"It's Only a Paper Moon," from *The Great Magoo* (Harburg, Rose and Arlen)

"If There is Someone Lovelier than You," from *Revenge with Music* (Schwartz and Dietz)

"A Foggy Day," from *A Damsel in Distress* (Ira and George Gershwin)

"Some Enchanted Evening," from *South Pacific* (Rodgers and Hammerstein)

While some lyrics embroider a theme of love, or—in many comedy songs—tell of personal unhappiness, or—as in charm songs—dance along in a happy, jaunty way, still others have a tale to tell.

The *narrative* lyric is set to the same formal musical patterns as all the others, but, as the lyrics require considerably more music than the others (since it has a story line to complete), the song results in several (as many as needed) choruses or verses-and-choruses in order to be able to complete the tale.

"The Surrey with the Fringe on Top," from *Oklahoma!* and "The Love of My Life," from *Brigadoon* are good examples of narrative lyrics. The first requires three verses (the third is spoken over music) and three choruses; the second needs a verse and four choruses, each separated by the verse, which has then become an "interlude," and a final interlude to complete the tale.

In the Ira Gershwin–Kurt Weill *Lady in the Dark* (1941), there are *two* narrative songs, "The Princess of Pure Delight" and "The Saga of Jenny." The first follows the traditional tale of a princess in search of a husband who will be chosen because he is able to solve a riddle. The lyrics are made of eight four-line stanzas, each followed by an amusing *spoken* line. (The music, incidentally, consists of eight-bar blocks, each followed by two bars to support each of the spoken lines. The form is an extension of the classical form, and is *A B A B C A B A*. This allows four *A*s instead of the usual three, three *B*s, and one *C*, which serves as a release since it is in contrast with both *A* and *B*.)

Also from *Lady in the Dark* is "The Saga of Jenny," which Ira Gershwin refers to as "a sort of blues bordello." The style of both words and music follow in the tradition of "Frankie and Johnny," "Cocaine Lil," and many others. The lyrical connection with the plot is clear since the heroine of the show, Liza Elliott, cannot make up her mind (her indecision is the show's central theme), and this is also Jenny's problem. The form consists of six sections, each sixteen bars long, and a coda, or ending.

Other examples of narrative songs are as follows:

"The Monkey in the Mango Tree," from *Jamaica* (Arlen and Harburg)

"Guess Who I Saw Today?" from *New Faces of 1952* (Grand and Boyd) (the narrative is completed in a single verse and a single chorus).

"Liaisons," from *A Little Night Music* (Sondheim)

"The Surrey with the Fringe on Top," from *Oklahoma!* (Rodgers and Hammerstein)

"The Red Ball Express," from *Call Me Mister* (Rome)

"Nothing," from *A Chorus Line* (Kleban and Hamlisch)

There is another kind of lyric that has little or no development but perpetuates itself through a series of shifting lyrical images. Cole Porter wrote a number of these. First, there is "The Physician," from *Nymph Errant* (1933). There are fourteen four-, five-, and six-line stanzas. The point of the song is that the physician admired many parts of the patient's body but never said he loved her. The "series" consists of the doctor's admiration of the patient's bronchial tubes, epiglottis, larynx, pharynx, and so on.

"Friendship," from *DuBarry Was a Lady* (1939), is another Cole Porter "series" song. There are five seven-line stanzas, and humor is created through the swift use of brief non sequiturs. The "list," or "series," consists of a number of "If you're ever in a . . ." and answered by what the singer (the friend) will do as a result. Porter uses another small device for humor at the conclusion of each section. The first one has at the end of the stanza "forgot" rhyming with "hot," then "forgit" with "it," "smoke" with "oke," and so on.

In "The Lady Is a Tramp" (Rodgers and Hart), from *Babes in Arms* (1937), the character singing about herself is enumerating her unfashionable, earthy tastes. These (a list) comprise the reasons for her being called "a tramp." But the lady and her reasons are simply substylish and categorize her as one who does not follow the dictates of fashion. In the verse, she describes herself as preferring simple food to more elaborate fare, hiking to attending the Beaux Arts Ball or knowing Noël Coward, and concluding, "My hobohemia is the place to be." In the two refrains and two encore refrains that follow, she dines early, comes to the theatre on time, sees only the people she likes, wouldn't shoot craps with the socially grand, go to Harlem elegantly dressed, or gossip with other girls. All of these are in the first two *A* sections of Refrain I (there are four refrains). The release (*B*) goes from negative to positive about what she likes: fresh wind in her hair, a life without care, and being broke doesn't bother her. The final *A* of Refrain I returns to her hates: cold, damp California, and so on. Other list examples include:

"Nobody's Chasing Me" (Cole Porter), from *Out of This World* (1950)

"Push de Button" (Arlen and Harburg), from *Jamaica* (1957)

"Nobody Makes a Pass at Me" (Harold Rome), in *Pins and Needles* (1937)

"The Impossible Dream" (Darion and Leigh), from *Man of La Mancha* (1965)

"Always True to You in My Fashion" (Cole Porter), from *Kiss Me Kate* (1949)

"Cherry Pies Ought to Be You" (Cole Porter), from *Out of This World* (1950)

"Yuletide, Park Avenue" (Harold Rome), from *Call Me Mister* (1946)

"Welcome Home" (Harold Rome), from *Fanny* (1954)

"My Mother's Wedding Day" (Lerner and Loewe), from *Brigadoon* (1947)

There are many different kinds of lyrics that end with "hooks," or "turnarounds," as they are sometimes called. This usually means that the last line of the song adds a new meaning, offers a surprise, or sheds new light on what has gone before.

As a first example I would point out Sheldon Harnick's "Far From the Home I Love," a song of farewell, from *Fiddler on the Roof* (1964). A daughter is leaving home to marry her loved one in Siberia. As she waits for the train with her father, she ponders the question of why she is going away, "far from the home I love?" but concludes the entire song with "Yet, there with my love, I'm home."

This switching around of nearly identical words imparts a

41

new meaning, one everybody can empathize with. The song is pointless without this line.

In Leonard Sillman's *New Faces of 1952*, there is a song "Guess Who I Saw Today?" by Murray Grand and Elisse Boyd, with a narrative lyric sung by a wife to her husband. The wife describes spending her day shopping, having difficulty finding a parking place, entering a small, dimly lit French café where she saw "two people at the bar who were so much in love." The final line of the song is "Guess who I saw today! I saw you!" This line not only completes the narrative but it *implies* that the wife very much loves her husband. Despite what she has observed, she is not angry but is perhaps hurt.

Walter Marks wrote a comedy song, which also is a narrative, for *Bajour* (1964). An academic-type girl is trying to locate any primitive tribe about which she can write a thesis. The song describes her imaginary unpleasant trek through African jungles, her joy at discovering (she thinks) a primitive tribe, and then her bitter disappointment at hearing the music of Bach, which tells her that Albert Schweitzer has already been there. The "joke" in this song is told by the music.

"Come with Me" (Lorenz Hart), from *The Boys from Syracuse* (1938), leads the listener to believe that the singer knows paradise: the rent is free, the landlord never bothers you, you have your own little room, and so on until the last line, "Come with me to jail."

Dorothy Fields wrote "I Dream Too Much" as the title song for a film in 1935. The refrain tells us that in dreams she experiences all the romantic things anyone could wish, but the final line turns us around: "Perhaps I dream too much alone."

Other examples of turnarounds, or hooks, are in: "I Love to Cry at Weddings" (Dorothy Fields), in *Sweet Charity* (1966); "Barcelona" (Stephen Sondheim), in *Company* (1970); and "Happiness" (Clark Gesner), in *You're a Good Man, Charlie Brown* (1967).

There are also lyrics that philosophize. Without making any comment on these individually, let me say that the best of them deal in *specific* images as opposed to general ones:

"You'll Never Walk Alone," from *Carousel* (Rodgers and Hammerstein—1945)

"The Impossible Dream," from *Man of La Mancha* (Darion and Leigh—1965)

"It Ain't Necessarily So," from *Porgy and Bess* (Ira and George Gershwin—1935)

"Yesterdays," from *Roberta* (Kern and Harbach—1933)

"The Eagle and Me," from *Bloomer Girl* (Harburg and Arlen—1944)

"Nickel Under the Foot," from *The Cradle Will Rock* (Blitzstein—1937)

"Old Man River," from *Show Boat* (Hammerstein and Kern—1927)

But philosophizing is not usually a function of song lyrics. It can lead to preaching, which is not an acceptable adjunct of theatre in any form. Morals may be implied, but never argued or even directly stated. The endings of the Chekhov plays contain good examples of nonpreaching but implied moralistic conclusions. There are many good reasons for avoiding lyrical philosophical flights. First, ideas must be expressed simply and briefly in songs, and philosophical exposition requires more time and space for such expression at any meaningful depth or development than is possible. What emerges then is too often only cliché. Then, too, philosophical lyrics seem to invite generalization: life, love, unhappiness, right, wrong, death, and so on, and good lyric-writing should deal in specific imagery much as the poetry of Emily Dickinson when she wrote of *small* things in a fresh, simple, original manner:

How dare the robins sing!

Nobody knows this little Rose—

Will there really be a "Morning"?

Until the Daffodil
Unties her yellow Bonnet

I'll tell you how the Sun rose—
A Ribbon at a time—

No matter how appropriate and specific lyric images are, they should also be organized. Helter-skelter imagery pulls the inner eye and the brain in too many different directions too *rapidly.*

I will illustrate good image organization in several songs. In every case, one image leads logically to another. Or a single locale contains several, and then another contains several others. There is always some unifying device.

Take, for example, "Some Enchanted Evening," from *South Pacific* (1949) by Rodgers and Hammerstein. The first *A* deals with seeing; the second with hearing; and the third with "finding and feeling." In Lerner and Loewe's "On the Street Where You Live," from *My Fair Lady* (1956), the first *A* is concerned with images on "the street," A^2 looks off into the trees and birds; *B* (in contrast) is about personal feeling, and in A^3 we are back again on "the street." In "If I Were a Rich Man," by Harnick and Bock from *Fiddler on the Roof* (1964), A^1 states the topic and A^2 the "no need to work"; B^1 describes the imaginary (rich) house, and B^2 the yard. Chorus II begins (A^1) with the topic; A^2, the "no need to work"; B^1, his wife under these conditions; *C*, the important men who will then come to him for advice; *B*, religion; A^1, the topic; A^2, the "no need to work"; and the coda (conclusion) is a question addressed to God as to why, after all, he couldn't be rich.

Since lyrics are meant to be heard and understood, it is my considered opinion that they should be simple. Monosyllabic words are preferable to polysyllabic ones. While rhymes—if they are fresh—contribute to a feeling of musicality, I recommend sacrificing clever rhyming—if a choice must be made—in favor of the clear development of a good idea.

One monotonous and needless miscalculation that many, especially new, lyricists make is to imply a stop at the end of every line, jingle-like.

> Mary had a little lamb
> Its fleece was white as snow. . . .

Most practiced writers often carry their thought *around* the end of the line, completing the thought somewhere in the next line, despite a rhyme which *seems* almost to be passed over at the end of the line.

There are many examples that could be cited from Shakespeare. One from *Romeo and Juliet:* Romeo speaks in Act II, Scene 2:

> . . . her eyes in heaven would through the airy region stream so
>   bright
> That birds would sing, and think it were not night.

Richard Wilbur's translations of Molière's plays into English verse seem to bypass the endless rhymed couplets of the original. The *sense* of the lines goes on in spite of rhymes, and this device is stimulating to the listener, not sleep-making as it might be.

From *Tartuffe*, Act IV, Scene 4:

> I'm going to act quite strangely now, and you
> Must not be shocked at anything I do.

If this is read (aloud) intelligently it would seem to be prose with only the passing rhyme-sound to lend a feeling of musicality.

Maurice Keller wrote in "The Orient Express," from *All the World—a Production:*

45

Plans for the fortification are missing. Some-
One who was guarding is eagerly kissing some-
One on the train.

In Rodgers and Hart's "Manhattan," from *Garrick Gaieties* (1925), rhymes are often positioned differently in adjacent lines, and this makes bypassing essential. Although the rhyme in the first two lines is Manhattan-Staten, it must be pointed out that the "too" at the end has two rhymes in the following line: "through" and "zoo."

Other examples in the works of many lyricists are numerous, although the following are cited for reference:

"Before I Kiss the World Goodbye," by Howard Dietz
"Yesterdays," by Otto Harbach
"I Feel a Song Comin' On," by Dorothy Fields
"Melinda," by Alan Jay Lerner
"The Little Things You Do Together," by Stephen Sond-
heim
"Now," by Stephen Sondheim

Since the lyric, like the music, is to be contained in the *A A B A* form, neither the lyric nor the line itself should be overlong, and the thoughts of the words, like the musical phrases, most often—though not necessarily—are divided into four-line quatrains, each section of which serves an eight-bar musical section.

The *B*, or release or bridge section, should, like the music, be in contrast—in point of view or however else that is possible—to the *A* ideas.

There are innumerable examples of these quatrains, none of which need to be quoted here. However, I recommend as models:

"Love for Sale" (Cole Porter)

"Bewitched, Bothered and Bewildered" (Rodgers and Hart)

"Some Enchanted Evening" (Rodgers and Hammerstein)

"My Ship" (Ira Gershwin and Kurt Weill)

"I Got Rhythm" (Ira and George Gershwin)

"By Myself" (Dietz and Schwartz)

"It's Only a Paper Moon" (E. Y. Harburg, with Rose and Arlen)

"I'm in the Mood for Love" (Dorothy Fields and Jimmy McHugh)

"Nobody Makes a Pass at Me" (Harold Rome)

"Joey, Joey, Joey" (Frank Loesser)

"Camelot" (Lerner and Loewe)

"Far from the Home I Love" (Harnick and Bock)

"They Say It's Wonderful" (Irving Berlin)

"I Feel Pretty" (Sondheim and Bernstein)

Written and printed lyrics can seem to contain longer or shorter lines or more or fewer lines than would seem to be suitable for the regular eight-bar musical phrase. Nevertheless, most of them are actually set to regular eight-bar musical phrases. For example, Cole Porter's "Always True to You in My Fashion" is written in five- and six-line stanzas. The musical form is *not* usual, although the eight-bar blocks are still used as the basis of this refrain. *A* is eight bars; then there is a kind of chorus-within-the-chorus containing the title line, which is also eight bars long. The entire layout of the refrain is:

A^1 (eight bars)

A^1 chorus answer (eight bars)

A^2 (eight bars)

A^2 chorus answer (eight bars)

B (eight bars)

A^3 chorus answer (eight bars)

The refrain, then, is forty-eight measures long.

On the other hand, Rodgers and Hart's "Here in My Arms" has eleven lines in the refrain, but Richard Rodgers' music sets it in the thirty-two-bar $A A B A$ form.

There are many examples of songs with lyrics that have fewer or more lines than would seem "standard," but the composer has usually managed to set them in the thirty-two-bar, $A A B A$ form.

It is recommended here that, at first, the usual form be adhered to, not only because it services the lyrics and the music well, but because this restriction will also serve as a means of funneling ideas succinctly and will probably prevent rambling in an improvisatory manner.

One facet which I have still to deal with is the lyrical differ-ence that characterizes the B section (or release) in a well-constructed song. I will cite several examples, which will by no means be exhaustive.

In Porter's "I Get a Kick Out of You," all three As concern getting "no kick" out of something, or something that others get a kick out of, but the B section tells us that he *does* get a kick out of her, although she "obviously doesn't adore me."

Rodgers and Hart's "My Funny Valentine" tells us in the first two As that he looks "laughable." B spells out his specific defects ("figure less than Greek," "mouth a little weak," and so on). The last A begs him not to change.

Ira Gershwin's words for "Someone to Watch Over Me" relate to "me," while the release tells us that "he" is not hand-some but "to my heart he'll carry the key."

In Schwartz and Dietz's "You and the Night and the Music," the first two A sections describe the effects of the title, while B considers the effects of "dancing" and "morning."

Harburg's lyric for "April in Paris" (three-line stanzas that musicalize to the regular eight-bar phrases) begins in the first two *A*s with the romantic feeling of the title, while *B* says that he never before knew the smile of spring, that his heart could never sing, he missed the warm embrace until—April in Paris.

The reader should read the releases (*B* sections) of the best theatre songs and he will nearly always find the topic treated in a different—sometimes reverse—manner or from another point of view.

THE PLACEMENT OF TITLES

Thought should be given to the placement of the song's title within the lyric. It is most often, though not invariably, heard in each *A* section, three times in the course of a single refrain. Sometimes *A* begins with the title or the title is used in the last line, but there is no rule. It may occur anywhere, but— wherever it occurs—it *is* clearly the title.

Some examples of placements of titles together with the number of times they are heard follow:

In "Where Is the Life That Late I Led?" (Porter), it is in the first line of the refrain and the last line of the whole song (twice).

In "The Physician" (Porter), it is in the first line, "Once I loved such a shattering physician. . . ." Although there are fourteen stanzas (four, five, and six lines), the word "physician" never recurs, but "he" is used constantly.

In "My Heart Belongs to Daddy" (Porter), with two *A A B A* choruses, it occurs at the end of the first two *A*s, in the first and third lines of *B*, and in the third (not fourth) line of the last *A* in Chorus I. In Chorus II, the identical pattern is repeated, except in the first *A* the last two lines are:

> Cause I can't be mean to Daddy
> 'Cause my da-da-daddy might spank!

Porter's "I Get a Kick Out of You" finds the title at the end of each of the three As.

In Rodgers and Hart's "Here in My Arms," the title occurs only at the start of the refrain and again at the start of the last A.

In Rodgers and Hart's "Manhattan," the word is treated as topic. (*All* titles are topics, but in this song the single word is the topic as opposed to other place names: Greenwich, Brighton, Yonkers, Coney, Bronx, Staten Island, and so on, and it is heard just enough to keep it alive as the very center of the song.) There are four refrains. "Manhattan" occurs in Refrain I in line 1 and in the next-to-final line; in Refrains II and III, in the next-to-final lines only. In Refrain IV, it is again (as in Refrain I) in the first and next-to-last lines.

In Rodgers and Hart's "There's a Small Hotel," it occurs only in the first and last lines.

In Hammerstein and Romberg's "Lover, Come Back to Me!" the title appears as the last line of each of the three As; however, at the end of the first A it is altered to "Lover, where can you be?"

In *Show Boat*, Hammerstein's lyric for "You Are Love" is set in a somewhat different musical form in which the refrain consists of three As—sixteen bars each—and contains no B. Of these three As, the second and third are nearly identical, whereas the first states the theme and then goes along in the song's sole difference. Each of the three As begin with "You are love . . . " "You are spring . . . "—and "You are love. . . ."

Ira Gershwin, who gave much conscious thought to titles and their placement, used them differently in almost every song. In "My Ship," the first two As begin with it; the last A, a six-line stanza, contains an altered version in the third line: "If the ship I sing."

In "Embraceable You," the title occurs in the second and

final lines of the refrain. In "Someone to Watch Over Me," it occurs at the end of each of the three *A*s. In "I Got Rhythm," Gershwin does something different. The first *A* begins with "I Got Rhythm," the second with "I got daisies." Other examples are too numerous to mention here, but can be observed in nearly all other theatre songs.

There are some songs whose titles *describe* the song, and in these instances the title never becomes a part of the lyrics. Examples: "Soliloquy," from *Carousel,* and "Adelaide's Lament," from *Guys and Dolls.*

There is one detail relating to the use of title in the lyrics of songs which should be pointed out. In many cases, the title line when it occurs at the end of each *A* is not made to rhyme *except* at the very end of the song. Perhaps the reason for this is that the rhyme-sound coming at the end gives a feeling of satisfaction and resolution. However, the reader should observe the practice in:

> "Embraceable You," by Ira and George Gershwin. The title rhymes only the last time with "do."
>
> "My Heart Stood Still," by Rodgers and Hart. There is a triple rhyme in the last line, "Un*til* the *thrill* of that moment when my heart stood *still.* "
>
> "Johnny One Note," by Rodgers and Hart. The embroidered last line is "Sing, Johnny One Note, out loud," which allows it to rhyme with "crowd" three lines earlier.
>
> "My Funny Valentine" ends, "Stay, little Valentine, stay!/Each day is Valentine's day."

Dorothy Fields, in "I Feel a Song Comin' On," saves the title rhyme until the end, rhyming it with "gone" in the preceding line.

Harold Rome's "To My Wife" rhymes the title only at the end, with "life" in the preceding line.

The inexperienced lyric writer must remember that whatever the musical form is to be, the usual—and in many ways the most helpful and difficult—is the $A\ A\ B\ A$ one. It should be obvious that in this form the three A sections must be provided with rhythmically matching words. This is to say that each line must correspond rhythmically and in length (number of poetic feet) with each other one: line 1 in A^1 must be equivalent to line 1 in A^2 and A^3, and so on, because it must match music which is similar if not identical.

LYRICS: ADVICE

In all best theatre lyrics rhymes are *perfect*, which is not a compliment, but a term. In today's popular music the use of imperfect rhymes doesn't seem to matter, but in the theatre, where good craftsmanship helps to keep the best shows afloat indefinitely and poor craftsmanship is up for reexamination again and again, it is not done. In songs that become popular —even *very* popular—for a more restricted period, temporary excitement and ear-splitting volume seem to outweigh all other considerations.

In the theatre, please do not attempt to rhyme plurals with singulars.

"Hat" and "cats" are not perfect rhymes.

In the same way, *m* does not rhyme with *n*.

"Claim" does not rhyme with "grain."

Present- and past-tense words do not rhyme.

"Called" does not rhyme with "fall."

Also, because much of our daily speech is so undisciplined, we tend to forget that many words have final consonants that too frequently go unnoticed. For that reason, the potential lyricist should be reminded that a word like "friend" does not rhyme with "men" unless the first of these words is employed colloquially as "frien'." There are too many of these accepted-unacceptables to begin to enumerate them all, but it is hoped that an alert writer will keep himself aware of them.

I would also caution the writer not to use words that are *not intended* to rhyme in close proximity to others that *nearly do* rhyme with something else, for example (at the end of three consecutive lines): tend, men, glen. My advice is to change the first one, "tend," to something with a totally different sound.

Also try to avoid the use of "love" at the end of a line. Remember that it has been used millions of times and that it only rhymes with "above," "glove," "dove," "shove," and "of." In fact, you will do yourself a great creative service if you learn to express the *meaning* of "love" without using the word altogether. It can be done.

Finally, I must urge both lyric writers and writers of dialogue for a musical show not to employ *rhymed dialogue* because it will seem to the listener that the composer refused, or forgot, to set it to music.

SINGING WORDS

Since the lyric writer *intends* to have his words sung, he should be aware of those separate sounds that melt together, those that do not (these serve their own purposes when they are employed intentionally), those that sing easily when applied to high notes, and those that sing best at the end of a song.

For words that "melt together," or fail to, one must consider the consonants that end and begin words that follow one another. There are so many problem sequences that I can only point out this basic idea. The following two words should be spoken aloud, and the writer will comprehend the problem.

"*That much.*" The final *t* of the first word must be articulated before going to the next consonant, and, if the words follow one another quickly, the teeth, tongue, and lips must work miracles. Also, there is no way that they can be said together. They do not "melt."

The following two combinations make similar problems: "took charge" and "dead set." Sounds like "going out" can be heard as "goin gout," which is far from desirable!

On the other hand, sequences like the following melt together: "walk on," "that time," and "dead tired." This is because after the *k* in the first example we have a word beginning with a vowel. After the *t* of "that" we have another *t*, and we normally enunciate it only once. It becomes "thatime" and the melting *sounds* clearly. In the case of "dead tired," the final *d* and the opening *t* are made by the tongue with a similar mechanism (try it) and what we readily accept in English speech is "deatired" because we understand it.

The other general danger (this is all put briefly, but my hope is that a talented writer will be sufficiently cautioned to carry on similarly on his own) occurs at the end of songs. The late Oscar Hammerstein II felt he had made an error at the end of "What's the Use of Wonderin' " in *Carousel* when he ended the song, "And all the rest is talk," because the singer (and the composer, usually) want the final note held, and with a word like "talk" the *k* should be articulated when sung as it is when it is spoken.

In fact, the best advice anyone can give a new lyricist and his composer is that the rhythm of song and the rhythm of speech should be as closely the same as possible. By definition, song is "elongated speech," so the question that naturally arises is "how elongated?" My answer is "not long," except . . .

This depends on vowel sounds. What has gone before has been largely related to consonants. The most open vocal sound is "ah," the next "oo." The sound that squeezes most, and one which should be avoided on high notes when the throat ought to be open, is "ee." The same principle applies in most cases to elongated words or syllables.

"Our Fa——ther who art in hea——ven" sings well with *Fa* and *hea* held longer than the other syllables.

No matter how popular it was, "Moon-li——ght on the Gan ——ges——" is terrible. The holding of "li" is not in itself bad because *i* is a diphthong and the knowledgeable singer will sing "LAH—eeght," but the "ght" to be enunciated later, is shocking, and Ganges can also be partly palatable because we hear "Ga—nges," but that "eez" held at the end of the phrase is an ugly sound.

Much of this is a matter of taste, which cannot be taught or even agreed upon. Each writer will have to come to grips with each problem himself, but I do suggest that lyrics be read *aloud* several times (if they are written prior to the music) before the composer works with them, so that he can better deal with whatever problems they may present.

COMEDY SONGS

Having discussed and given examples earlier of ballad and charm songs, I will next take up the most illusive variety—the *comedy song*—which makes audiences laugh now and for a long time after; if it fails in this respect, it cannot be so categorized.

For want of a better word, let us use "joke" to indicate the explosive payoff of a funny song. But to avoid confusion, it must be understood that no ordinary joke—not even the very best one—can be used as the basis of a comedy song because any tellable joke seems to have been told by everyone in the world within an amazingly brief time-space. Once it has been heard, it is dead: no one wants to hear it again.

The "joke" in a comedy song should be generated out of situation and character. Usually it is meaningless if repeated out of context, and if it works well it will continue to be funny for an indefinite time.

For example, is it possible to elicit laughter or even a smile from someone who has not seen *My Fair Lady* if you are foolish enough to tell him about "I'm an Ordinary Man"? What makes that song amusing is the audience's observation of Professor Higgins, his character, his selfishness, and his failure to understand other human beings. Similarly, "Adelaide's Lament" in *Guys and Dolls* is amusing only when you know Adelaide's background and her relationship with Nathan Detroit, as well as the incident that provokes the song (Nathan's failure to keep a date with Adelaide). All this is revealed again in the lyrics of "Adelaide's Lament," but the all-important setup in the show itself is missing if the song is presented outside of the show; therefore, *telling* the humor of the song to anyone who has not seen the show will fail to convey any meaning.

Some examples of comedy songs from the theatre are:

"I Cain't Say No," from *Oklahoma!* (Rodgers and Hammerstein)

"To Keep My Love Alive," from *A Connecticut Yankee* (Rodgers and Hart)

"Adelaide's Lament," from *Guys and Dolls* (Loesser)

"The Love of My Life," from *Brigadoon* (Lerner and Loewe)

"You Must Meet My Wife," from *A Little Night Music* (Sondheim)

"Do You Love Me?" from *Fiddler on the Roof* (Bock and Harnick)

"Chysanthemum Tea," from *Pacific Overtures* (Sondheim)

"I'm an Ordinary Man," from *My Fair Lady* (Lerner and Loewe)

"Bewitched, Bothered and Bewildered," from *Pal Joey* (Rodgers and Hart)

Now, there are certain facets that these songs have in common. Most of them are plaints. The character who sings them is unhappy or discontented. More than that, she (he) is sincere and naive, and she is speaking about herself, her unfortunate lot, and in the *first person*.

It generally comes as a surprise to people who have not previously thought seriously about it to learn that laughter is to be found in *unhappy situations.*

In *Oklahoma!* Ado Annie's certainty that something terrible in her nature prevents her refusing a man's attempts to kiss her is, to her, a serious matter. In *A Connecticut Yankee*, the singer describes the murder of her husbands "to keep my love alive." In *Brigadoon*, Meg Brockie is in search of a husband. Without her own awareness of the reasons why she has thus far failed, she tells us of her father's eagerness to be rid of her —hence her persistent attempts, and her overzealousness, which has driven each prospective husband away.

In *A Little Night Music*, "You Must Meet My Wife" is funny at first because the hero is sincere in enumerating his young wife's good qualities, while at the same time his former mistress is agreeing with his appraisal, though sarcastically: nearly identical words take on opposite meanings. Also, in a sense, the husband sings out of a kind of desperation: he has really come to his former friend because he is sex-starved and this "preamble" to what he hopes will follow is a kind of attempt to salve his own conscience by "speaking" so glowingly of his virgin-wife.

In *Fiddler on the Roof*'s duet "Do You Love Me?" Tevye, the father-husband and leading character, has just given his blessing (he was not asked his permission) to the forthcoming marriage of his second daughter. He wonders how he will explain this to his ill-tempered wife, Golde. As he encounters her, Tevye suddenly is possessed of a new idea to distract her—an idea very foreign to their lives but very closely akin to the reason his second daughter is to marry a poor student. He asks (sings) "Do you love me?" changing the subject hilariously and stunning his wife. A bad situation becomes a funny and charming one, also an unexpected one.

In "Chysanthemum Tea," a Japanese mother is serving poisoned tea to her ineffectual son. Throughout the song, with its long array of amusing rhymes, the son becomes weaker and weaker and finally dies.

During the blessed days of silent films, America produced some of the greatest of clowns: Chaplin, Keaton, W. C. Fields, Conklin, Lloyd, Turpin—and later the Marx Brothers, Laurel and Hardy, and many others. Most of them never smiled. We laughed at their difficulties and misfortunes.

In trying to translate this kind of material into words, there are major problems. As in trying to discuss comedy songs, we produce no laughter when we try to describe what these silent clowns did. Their faces' reacting to their unhappiness is what made us laugh. They "spoke" of themselves. We almost never make people laugh when we try telling them of something we saw that struck us as humorous.

Successful comedy is highly personal. It is this personal experience that must be related in words (lyrics), and that experience is wide-eyed and unselfconscious. It appeals to the listener for understanding and sympathy. It is the only time in the theatre when self-pity can be even bearable, for when self-pity takes itself seriously we become bored, just as we are bored with it in life. Comedy does not engender pity. If we want pity, there is an opposite way of eliciting it, and we will discuss that next.

The comedy song, then, finds its subject matter in personal dissatisfaction, or even in misery. Of course, in translating this material into lyric form, there must be careful organization (as in the successful telling of a joke): we must sound sober, and attractive rhymes can help enormously to increase the laughter. Actually, if we create a consistent rhyme scheme, we may succeed in *predicting* it just ahead of the laugh, and this can enhance the result.

There are three important sections that—added together—comprise the shape of the comedy lyric: the setup, the development, and the payoff. Each functions exactly as its name implies. The setup introduces a situation. The situation is developed until it is resolved—unexpectedly, in a comedy song—in the payoff. Consider any ordinary joke and you will observe these three stages.

Now, unless there is a satisfactory payoff to a comedy song —and this must occur at the very end of it—the song is not funny. That being the case, it follows that in writing a comedy song the lyricist must begin working from the end. He must have a clear idea of the subject matter, but he must know in advance of writing the lyrics how the song is to end. If he does know that, he will work backward until all three of its necessary stages are expressed in proper order.

In general, there are two kinds of comedy songs: one that I call the "short joke" form, and the other, the "long joke" form. In the short joke, the three steps (setup, development, and payoff) occur in each eight bars and there are then four jokes in each thirty-two-bar refrain. An example of this is to be found in Rodgers and Hart's "Bewitched, Bothered and Bewildered," from *Pal Joey*. In the long joke, the real payoff occurs at the end of each refrain, or once in thirty-two bars. There may be *additional* laughs during the refrain but there *must* be one at the end. An example of this is to be found in Lerner and Loewe's "The Love of My Life" in *Brigadoon*.

In these two classical examples, there are additional things to be pointed out. In "Bewitched, Bothered and Bewildered," that phrase—"Bewitched, bothered and bewildered am I"—(sometimes slightly altered at its end) occurs at the end of each *A* section right *after* the joke or payoff. It then serves as a cushion. After the audience has heard it once, it can laugh through the others knowing that it will not be missing the next setup. (There are five sets of lyrics.)

In "The Love of My Life," the verse occurs before each of the four refrains, and again after the last (five times in all). The character's naiveté is clearly stated because in each of these she tells *us* that she told her Pa how she lost the last "love" and Pa keeps telling her she must look again. This spells out the fact —unnoticed and unrecognized by the girl herself—that Pa wants to be rid of her. Also, Choruses I and II are related to one another in that the romantic candidate in Chorus II heard about her from her candidate in Chorus I. Choruses III and IV are also related because the man in III is a poet and the one in IV is a soldier, and in IV she comments, "The sword has more might than the pen."

In a sense, all emotional results—comic or sad—are due to the workings of what I call a "triangle." One side of this is the "situation" which the audience has seen developing. The second side is the "song" (or soliloquy) which, while it is a part of the situation, nevertheless reacts in its own way *antithetically*. The third side is the "audience," with its reaction to this interplay.

Now, exactly what do I mean by the song's reacting "antithetically" to the situation? In the comedy song—already demonstrated—the reaction against the sad situation is not the performer's reaction but the one that is transferred to the audience. In the song that engenders a feeling of sadness, the most effective song works *optimistically* in the face of the situation. In this way, once again, the emotion (now sad) is transferred to the audience.

Before giving examples that may clarify this principle, let me caution the writer (as well as the performer) that *if he feels everything* the audience will feel nothing, for there will be nothing left for it to feel. This kind of song or performance then becomes a spectacle in the same sense as—let us say—when a person in public becomes noisily grief-stricken: we are appalled at the sight, but not moved. On the other hand, when we encounter someone we know who has cause for grief and who behaves stoically, we are very apt to suffer the emotion which, at least on the outside, appears to be absent.

SAD SONGS

Having outlined the nature of the comedy song, I would like to proceed to the opposite end of the spectrum and speak about the sad song. It might be as well to remind the reader here that most songs are soliloquies. The comedy song is a personal soliloquy about misfortune or something in that general area. The song that would have a truly sad effect on an audience must be optimistic in tone if the audience is to empathize with the singer.

In Euripides' *Iphigenia in Aulis,* since the Greek fleet has been unable to sail to wage war on Troy because there has been no wind, Agamemnon, the king, has been advised by the prophet Calchas that, in order to have winds for sailing and a victory in Troy, he must sacrifice his daughter Iphigenia. To get his daughter to come to him, Agamemnon has sent a letter, saying that she is to come at once to marry Achilles.

Wife and daughter arrive in a highly celebrative mood, but Agamemnon must eventually reveal the truth. At that time, in a long scene, the mother and daughter, groveling at his feet, plead with Agamemnon not to go through with his plan.

We are not moved by this, although we feel regret, terror, fear, and many other things. The moment of being moved comes when Iphigenia has a gradual change of heart. She speaks:

To Greece I give this body of mine
Slay it in sacrifice and conquer Troy
These things coming to pass, Mother, will be
A remembrance for years. They will be
My children, my marriage; through the years
My good name and my glory. It is
A right thing that Greeks rule barbarians,
Not barbarians Greeks.*

There is more. All of it is emotionally devastating to the other characters in the play, as well as to the audience. Euripides has used every device of selflessness in Iphigenia! She does not want her mother to accompany her to her death, she begs her mother to look after her brother Orestes, she begs her mother not to hate her father, and so on. But she says nothing about her own sad plight.

We are familiar with the double suicide of Romeo and Juliet in Shakespeare's play. Strangely, we are not moved by the two acts of death. What we are moved by comes *after*, first when the prince (arbiter between the Capulets and Montagues) says:

Capulet, Montague,
See what a scourge is laid upon your hate,
That heaven finds means to kill your joys with love!

Later both parents extend hands in friendship, which they had previously been unable to do, and in doing so now, we weep because this reconciliation comes too late to save the lives of their children.

In *King Lear,* near the end of the play, Lear enters with the dead body of his daughter Cordelia in his arms. His grief is terrible but still has less "effect" than his momentary hope that she is still alive.

At the end of *Othello,* having stabbed himself after murdering his wife, Othello says

*Euripides, *Iphigenia in Aulis,* trans. Charles R. Walker (Chicago: University of Chicago Press, 1958, 1959).

I kiss'd thee ere I kill'd thee,
No way but this—
Killing myself to die upon a kiss.

It is not the fact of Othello's death that disturbs us emotionally, but this image of dying upon a kiss.

Near the finish of Peter Shaffer's *The Royal Hunt of the Sun,* Pizzaro has ordered the Inca emperor Atahuallpa killed. The emperor had believed himself born of the sun and therefore deathless. As the aged Pizzaro is left sitting beside the body of the young dead emperor, natives sing a Chant of Resurrection. But the emperor does not revive. The sun rises and Pizzaro in grief exclaims as he slaps the dead body:

Cheat! You've cheated me! Cheat. . . . You have no eyes for me now, Atahuallpa: they are dusty balls of amber I can tap on. You have no peace for me, Atahuallpa: the birds still scream in your forest. You have no joy for me, Atahuallpa, my boy: the only joy is in death. . . . And yet you saw once. The sky sees nothing, but you saw. Is there comfort there? The sky knows no feeling, but we know them, that's sure.

Then Pizzaro sings a little song that ends the play:

See, see the fate, O little finch
Of robber birds, O little finch.

The same devices are at work in all of the best tragedies— the end of Arthur Miller's *Death of a Salesman,* Tennessee Williams' *A Streetcar Named Desire, Hamlet* (see Ophelia's first mad song), Chekhov's *The Cherry Orchard,* and many, many others. The character—speaking or singing—must not bear the entire grief: it must be transferred to, and borne by, the audience.

In musical theatre, the same principle applies. See the end of *Carousel;* the end of *West Side Story;* "Far from the Home I Love," from *Fiddler on the Roof;* "Un Bel Di," from *Madame Butterfly;* Violetta's death in the opera *La Traviata* and Camille's, in Dumas' play of the same name; the trio from Act III of *Der Rosenkavalier;* and the"Liebestod" from *Tristan und Isolde.*

Notice that, in every one of these examples, the effect of poignance occurs (or begins to occur) at the moment when, in the face of tragedy, there is a bright afterglow.

Of course, none of this is new, this optimism in the face of death or disaster. The twentieth-century dramatists, however, probably contributed something to its reemployment that had virtually disappeared after Shakespeare, and especially through the treacherous nineteenth century, when sentimentality threatened to choke the life out of everything.

The musical numbers listed above (and many others) from opera and musical shows are moving. Note that the music for all of them is written in *major* keys.

The clue here is the projection of a brighter future in the midst of tragedy or despair.

OPENINGS

The opening of a musical—perhaps also the opening of a play—is of such importance to everything that follows that it is nearly impossible to tell what is needed until the work is entirely, or at least nearly, finished.

Early musicals had no such problem since these were governed by convention. Nearly every show opened with a song and dance that had little more to do with the show than did the introductions to Josef Haydn's symphonies. They proved at once, if anyone in the audience harbored any doubts, that there were pretty girls and handsome boys and that the evening was to be weightless. And very often these girls and boys further relieved the onlookers of any need to exercise their own mental powers by identifying for them the locale and the period of the show. Of course, otherwise, no one could have guessed, since the girls and boys were costumed to represent the people they were loosely impersonating and the scenery that backed them up most graphically took care of communicating time and place.

The only real accomplishment in all of this—persisting as it did from show to show for thirty or forty years—was, as in the introduction to the Haydn symphonies, that it helped to cover the noisy seating of latecomers. Afterward, the show (and the symphony) got underway. In short, these openings were only appendages to the shows, not integral parts.

While *Show Boat* (1927) followed the formula common to all shows of that time, it added another dimension through the greater importance of the music. Also, two choruses—one white and one black—represented a significant innovation that was to become a unique feature of the show itself. *Porgy and Bess* (1935) opened (at least on paper, although I think it was cut out of the actual first production) with a long, bluesy section that was intended to set the mood. When it was excised, the opera opened (serendipity at work) with the dreamy ballad "Summertime," which provided a jumping-off place for what was to become a very busy and intensely dramatic Act I, Scene 1.

With few other important exceptions, it was *Pal Joey* (1941) which began a fairly steady practice of relating openings to the musical play that followed. In this show, Joey, our heel-hero, was simply auditioning for a job in a small nightclub. He sang part of a "throw-away" song to the accompaniment of an onstage piano. Very plainly, though he can neither sing nor dance very well, we know he has a considerable amount of chutzpah. After *Pal Joey*, the kinds, qualities, and functions of openings took their varied places in history.

There was the solo ballad, "Oh, What a Beautiful Morning," in *Oklahoma!*; a pantomine scene, introducing the principal characters, played out to a suite of waltzes in *Carousel*; non-

65

musical openings in *Kiss Me, Kate* and *The King and I;* followed
not too long after the shows got under way with "Another
Openin', Another Show" and "I Whistle a Happy Tune,"
respectively. *South Pacific* has a small delicate song "Dites-
Moi" for two children. *The Most Happy Fella*, after some under-
scored dialogue, has a comedy song, "Ooh, My Feet," sung by
a secondary character. *Fiddler on the Roof,* after a small violin
cadenza in lieu of an overture, begins with a monologue given
by its principal character, followed by his singing of "Tradition," which includes his comments as an introduction to all
of the other characters in the show. *A Little Night Music* begins
with an "overture" about remembering sung by a "Greek
chorus" of five (three women and two men) in evening clothes.
A Funny Thing Happened on the Way to the Forum opens with
"Comedy Tonight," sung by its star and two members of the
male ensemble. *Wonderful Town* starts with "Christopher
Street," during which a guide shows two tourist couples
around Greenwich Village, where they see an ensemble of
village "types"; then, two by two, all of the minor characters
in the oncoming show are introduced wittily, for this is to be
a comedy.

My Fair Lady begins as a play—as Shaw's *Pygmalion,* to be
exact. There are nearly seven printed pages of dialogue during
which one meets the three principal characters, so we know
fairly well what they are like and the professions of the two
main ones, and are brought head-on to the differences between
them that create their and the show's chief conflict. After all
of that, there is the first musical number "Why Can't the
English?" (teach their children how to speak), which sets up
everything that is to follow.

Company opens with a "surprise" birthday party given by
five couples (the close and caring friends of the central character). There is no song—the scene introduces all of them, including Bobby, the main character, and shows the friends'

concern for Bobby and their petty irritations with one another. All of this is important to the show as a whole.

A Chorus Line begins with a choreographer-director facing a stageful of dancers—"hopefuls" prepared to audition for a new show. The director, with his assistant, demonstrates "combinations"—movement designs—and, four by four, the dancers go through their paces, some of them performing fairly accurately, others less well. *A Chorus Line* is the only musical I recall that opens with dancing that is meaningful.

These examples are more than enough to demonstrate the variety of successful (workable) musical show openings. In many different ways, all of them helped to usher onto the stage what was or is to follow.

Experience has taught me that the best openings of musicals are written, *even conceived,* after the show has been finished. In many of the above cases, that which we have eventually come to know as the opening was actually a replacement for what was originally written.

I don't think it is a digression to introduce here an idea of mine—that Shakespeare, whose plays are models of libretto writing, could not possibly have begun many of his plays with what we know today as the opening. Could a writer who had not seen Shakespeare's *entire* play—from start to finish—have written the "chorus" that begins *Romeo and Juliet,* which, in fourteen lines, spells out for us both the entire play and a clear statement of theme? Could *any* writer have begun *Macbeth* with the little trio of witches ("When shall we three meet again?") which introduces these creatures and *names* the chief character?

Consider the first scene of *Hamlet.* Nothing happens in it that is not *described* after the fact in the following scene. Strictly speaking, its only necessity lies in its casting an all-important mood of suspense over the early part of the following court scene (Scene 2); without it, the scene might seem flat.

(This suspense is what works so well in the first scene of Stoppard's play *Rosencrantz and Guildenstern Are Dead*.) In all these Shakespeare works and in many others, the plays themselves actually commence in the scene following their openings.

My advice to new writers is to create whatever "gangplank" they feel is necessary in order for *them* to get into their show, but to leave any serious consideration of a permanent "opening" until much later on, when, in structuring the whole thing, they will have a clearer picture of what the show's opening should be.

If I may be allowed an analogy: an architect does not begin structuring a house by designing a front door. Size, proportion, style, and many other elements have to be decided first.

One last word about a musical show opening: it must help to define the entire show. With that in mind, please study the aforementioned openings and their relationships to their shows.

SONG MOVEMENT

In general—though it is not considered often enough—there are two types of songs: reflective and active. Each is determined by what is indicated in the lyrics.

A reflective song is inactive; that is, the lyrics do not suggest action. Instead, there is mood—often suggested and supported by the music—an inner sense of development, sadness, happiness, and so on. If used too frequently in a theatre score, this kind of song can become nontheatrical. The visual aspect, what the audience sees, must be "invented" by the singing actor and/or the stage director. The music, face, and body "act," but they have no place to go.

Nearly all of Shakespeare's soliloquies are reflective, sometimes with one development at the end that suggests future action. With this important addition, they become active. Hamlet's first soliloquy is wholly reflective: "O! that this too too solid flesh would melt" ends "But break my heart, for I must hold my tongue"—grief and inaction.

However, in Act II, Hamlet's big aria, which begins "Now I am alone," develops, becomes tempestuous, and ends, after anticipating the play that he will present, with "The play's the thing/Wherein I'll catch the conscience of the King"—resolve to action.

In the musical theatre there are many songs in both categories. The music may sometimes be active and the lyrics reflective. For example, "Glitter and Be Gay" from *Candide* (Bernstein and Wilbur) is satirical, the music is largely swift and light, but the lyrics are humorously reflective. On the other hand, "Come to Me, Bend to Me" from *Brigadoon* (Lerner and Loewe) has quiet, delicate music but the lyrics "travel" and suggest action.

The reason for calling attention to these dual categories relates wholly to the theatre. The staging of a *reflective* song requires a good deal of tasteful creativity on the part of the singer as actor, and on the stage director's inventiveness. Without both—*suggested* by the lyrics—the rendition of the song can become static and nontheatrical.

On the other hand, the *active* song suggests its own movement by the images presented in the lyrics. While the singer still must act the song (all songs), the stage director need only present, rather than invent, the course of action spelled out in the lyrics.

If the reader studies the *lyrics* of the following songs (listed in both categories) he will understand what I mean. This list could be endless.

REFLECTIVE

"Where or When" *(Babes in Arms)*, Rodgers and Hart, 1937
"My Funny Valentine" *(Babes in Arms)*, Rodgers and Hart, 1937
"The Face on the Dime" *(Call Me Mister)*, Rome, 1946
"Glitter and Be Gay" *(Candide)*, Bernstein and Wilbur, 1956
"Mira" *(Carnival)*, Bob Merrill, 1961
"The Ladies Who Lunch" *(Company)*, Sondheim, 1970
"My Heart Stood Still" *(A Connecticut Yankee)*, Rodgers and Hart, 1927
"Fanny" *(Fanny)*, Rome, 1954
"Sunrise, Sunset" *(Fiddler on the Roof)*, Bock and Harnick, 1964
"You Are Beautiful" *(Flower Drum Song)*, Rodgers and Hammerstein, 1958
"Diamonds Are a Girl's Best Friend" *(Gentlemen Prefer Blondes)*, Styne and Robins, 1949
"Bidin' My Time" *(Girl Crazy)*, the Gershwins, 1930
"More I Cannot Wish You" *(Guys and Dolls)*, Loesser, 1950
"Little Lamb" *(Gypsy)*, Styne and Sondheim, 1959
"I Believe in You" *(How to Succeed in Business Without Really Trying)*, Loesser, 1961
"The Most Beautiful Girl in the World" *(Jumbo)*, Rodgers and Hart, 1935
"Hello, Young Lovers" *(The King and I)*, Rodgers and Hammerstein, 1951
"So in Love" *(Kiss Me, Kate)*, Porter, 1948
"My Ship" *(Lady in the Dark)*, Weill and Gershwin, 1949
"Cry the Beloved Country" *(Lost in the Stars)*, Weill and Anderson, 1949
"Dulcinea" *(Man of La Mancha)*, Leigh and Darion, 1965
"Joey, Joey, Joey" *(The Most Happy Fella)*, Loesser, 1956

ACTIVE

"Where Is the Tribe for Me" *(Bajour)*, Marks, 1964

"Anything You Can Do (I Can Do Better)" *(Annie Get Your Gun)*, Irving Berlin, 1946

"The Eagle and Me" *(Bloomer Girl)*, Harburg and Arlen, 1944

"Come with Me" *(The Boys from Syracuse)*, Rodgers and Hart, 1938

"I'll Go Home with Bonnie Jean" *(Brigadoon)*, Lerner and Loewe, 1947

"Come to Me, Bend to Me" *(Brigadoon)*, Lerner and Loewe, 1947

"Wait Till You See Her" *(By Jupiter)*, Rodgers and Hart, 1942

"You're Just in Love" *(Call Me Madam)*, Berlin, 1950

"The Red Ball Express" *(Call Me Mister)*, Rome, 1946

"Being Alive" *(Company)*, Sondheim, 1970

"Another Hundred People" *(Company)*, Sondheim, 1970

"Nickel Under the Foot" *(The Cradle Will Rock)*, Blitzstein, 1938

"Art for Art's Sake" *(The Cradle Will Rock)*, Blitzstein, 1938

"Soliloquy" *(Carousel)*, Rodgers and Hammerstein, 1945

"Far from the Home I Love" *(Fiddler on the Roof)*, Bock and Harnick, 1964

"When I'm Not Near the Girl I Love" *(Finian's Rainbow)*, Lane and Harburg, 1947

"Lazy Afternoon" *(The Golden Apple)*, Moross and Latouche, 1954

"Luck Be a Lady Tonight" *(Guys and Dolls)*, Loesser, 1950

"Rose's Turn" *(Gypsy)*, Styne and Sondheim, 1959

"Hello, Dolly!" *(Hello, Dolly!)*, Jerry Herman, 1964

"Papa, Won't You Dance with Me" *(High Button Shoes)*, Styne and Cahn, 1947

"Spring Is Here" *(I Married an Angel)*, Rodgers and Hart, 1938

"I Whistle a Happy Tune" *(The King and I)*, Rodgers and Hammerstein, 1951

"The Impossible Dream" *(Man of La Mancha)*, Leigh and Darion, 1966

"Happy to Make Your Acquaintance" *(The Most Happy Fella)*, Loesser, 1956

While good songs in both groups serve valuable purposes, those with more active lyrics are, in my opinion, more theatrical. Reflective songs, useful in the theatre for a variety of purposes, are more easily performed away from the stage, under nontheatrical conditions, and usually with great success.

3

The Libretto

THE CREATION OF A BOOK or libretto of a musical show is still (in 1977) one of the most elusive problems of a theatrical undertaking. The Twenties and Thirties brought into the theatre many wonderful and enduring songs which were made to go with books that were barely serviceable in their own times, were brushed aside by the critics as predictably foolish, and died shortly after their birth, leaving a great heritage of music and lyrics to go wandering about—showless—forever. When shows ran a season, they suffered no financial loss. Stars were abundant then because, in those pre-TV times, they were made by and lived by Broadway, and movies for the most part created and exploited their own special stars.

The songs and the stars and the lavish productions seem to have been enough. The first musical that had a durable book inhabited by human beings was *Porgy and Bess* (1935), but it was not as successful in its own time as many other lesser and now-long-forgotten works.

Today, with a more demanding, perhaps more intellectual or better educated audience in the theatre, the book has become an element of prime importance. The music and lyrics are integral parts of it, as are the expert dancing and the sophisticated and visually simpler productions.

Since about 1940 the superior musicals—the ones with literate books and good scores—seem to have achieved an unending life. The best ones are great successes and are enjoyed universally. Many less-than-best ones are also successful for a time, and these, too, usually draw the biggest audiences everywhere in the world.

These successful libretti are adaptations from plays—some with a history of success, others out-and-out failures—novels, films, short stories, biographies, or histories. Attempts at original libretti have almost always failed. Why, I do not know, but I do know that the history of the musical theatre from the earliest times (opera, operetta, and the others) is also the history of adaptation. The Greek plays were taken from mythology and history. Audiences in attendance knew the plots intimately ahead of time. The Mystery and Miracle plays were adaptations of stories from the Bible or the lives of saints; though all were theatrically embroidered, plotwise they were well known. Shakespeare created no new plots. Opera, from the very beginning, took its characters and situations from mythology and history, and later librettists based their works on the plays and novels of the most successful writers: Beaumarchais, Dumas, Hugo, Shakespeare, Corneille, Pushkin, Goethe, and many others.

What, then, is a good libretto? That, too, is a complicated question, but I shall try to answer it. A good libretto has always contained a fairly simple story line with which audiences can identify. Usually there is at least one subplot. The three-dimensional characters are prototypes without (hopefully) being stereotypes, which means that they are easily iden-

74

tifiable, uncomplicated, and easy for audiences to relate to, without being ordinary and stale. The situations, by being recognizable, invite empathy, contain the kind of material that can be sung about, laughed with, and perhaps wept over. Above everything, the characters and situations must have the capacity to generate, and to sustain, interest from the beginning to the very end. It is a mistake to think that audiences go to theatrical performances in order to see "how things turn out." They attend and remain only when their interest is held throughout. The ending is usually predictable.

The characters and situations must be specific. Mrs. Anna *(The King and I)* is not just any schoolteacher. Eliza Doolittle *(My Fair Lady)* is not just any ignorant London flower-seller. Desirée *(A Little Night Music)* is not just any still-attractive middle-aged actress. All have something special about them, but all relate to other schoolteachers, street peddlers, and actresses. Their special qualities attract attention; their general class, which allows everyone to relate to them, holds that attention.

This fairly well, if not completely, describes what I believe constitutes a good libretto, with one enormous exception: it must arouse *feeling* so that the audience cares for the people and what happens to them every step of the way, even though many know in advance exactly how things will turn out. No one can help knowing at the outset that *West Side Story* will end catastrophically, but the show engages us throughout, and that is what matters. (In *Romeo and Juliet,* its progenitor, Shakespeare tells us at the very outset exactly how things will turn out.) Also, the catastrophe will engender a conclusion that will touch us far more than the catastrophe itself.

Libretti are hard to come by. Not all good playwrights have as yet come to grips with the vast differences between a good play and a good libretto. In all theatre, however, there is a large element of uncertainty, and even writers with great experience and talent have failures. No show has been finished until it has been experienced by an audience. After that, the people involved in the show's creation usually have a clearer idea of what they have accomplished and what they have failed to do.

It follows, then, that the most successful librettists (few in number) are in great demand, and new composers and lyricists are going to find it impossible to persuade successful librettists to spend a year or two collaborating with them on original material when the chances are that such librettists have what at least appear to be "safer" projects offered them by reputable collaborators, with established producers who will pay them something in advance for their work.

What, then, does the new composer/lyricist do? In my opinion, he must learn to create, from a play, film, or novel, scene-by-scene synopses for which he can create his songs. If writers are able to place characters in specific situations, they have most of what they require in order to write the better part of a score. With synopsis and score, they have at least the beginnings of a project that they can audition for potential librettists, directors, and producers. If they are successful, the librettist's ultimate creation will quite possibly require some songs that are different from the ones originally created, but that is a minor consideration. Music and lyrics can be written quickly if the writer knows his craft. Work on a libretto requires much more time.

In my own experience, I have seen a number of eventually successful shows begin this way, and I propose now to point out a very general way of creating a scene-by-scene synopsis. First, however, it would be wise to examine other musicals reduced here to synopses and compare them as musicals with their original source material.

One last word before embarking on what I believe is this all-important project. We constantly read or hear that a musical has, or has not, been "faithful to the original." I urge everyone to ignore such remarks, as they are beside the real point, which is: "Does the musical work?" With the exception of *My Fair Lady*, I know of no successful musical that did not involve considerable turning around of the original material, cutting out and/or adding characters, opening up the proscenium to *show* much of what is only *spoken about* in the original. All of this, I hope, will become more lucid with the following presentations.

One bit of advice concerning the choice of material with which to work. Many previously unsuccessful plays may very well be prime candidates for adaptation because the reason for their failure might have been the lack of some vital ingredient. Other possibilities are once-successful plays that now seem old-fashioned. In both cases, the introduction of music and the shifting about of the original form so that the music can be properly integrated may be just what is needed to make them viable now.

Lynn Riggs' play *Green Grow the Lilacs* ran 64 performances in 1931, and beginning in 1943 its musical version—*Oklahoma!*—ran 2248 performances!

Also, in the case of a play that is far less than a masterpiece, adaptors can feel free to change, cut, and insert new material, whereas with a classic or a well-known, highly respected play, adaptors must be careful and discreet about tampering with it. Sidney Howard's *They Knew What They Wanted* was an old-fashioned play that had virtually fallen into discard when Frank Loesser undertook enchanting it as *The Most Happy Fella*. He began the musical two scenes ahead of the play's beginning, and provided considerably more, visually and emotionally, than the play did.

When Arthur Laurents wrote "Jerome Robbins' concept" as *West Side Story*, a masterpiece was being dealt with: *Romeo and Juliet*, restructured. However, the original was "interpreted" so that the Montagues and Capulets became the Sharks and the Jets, rival street gangs—more parental than parents. The place became New York City as opposed to "fair Verona"; the time, the present. Shakespeare provided the theme, the plot, and the basic characters, but *West Side Story* achieved its own identity and was not simply a rehash.

Likewise, Shaw's *Pygmalion*, after much cutting, became *My Fair Lady*. Many of Shaw's ideas were transformed into songs. Twice we were shown Doolittle—Eliza's father—with two drinking companions outside his neighborhood pub. We saw Ascot, the Embassy Ball, the Flower Market at Covent Garden, and the exterior of Higgins' house ("On the Street Where You Live"). The sequence of events in Shaw's play was retained, however, despite cutting and the insertion of new scenes.

Let us next compare the principal characters of several musical adaptations with the original ones and observe the differences.

Oklahoma!/Green Grow the Lilacs

Will Parker (romantic opposite of Ado Annie) is created in the musical. He is mentioned once in *Green Grow the Lilacs*.

Jud (Jeeter in the play) is humanized in the single song Rodgers and Hammerstein wrote for him: "Lonely Room."

Ado Annie in the musical is sexy, vivacious, *gamine*. The following is Riggs' description of her in his play: "She is an unattractive, stupid-looking farm girl . . . her dress is of red gingham, and very unbecoming."

Carousel/Liliom

Marie in Molnár's *Liliom* became *Carrie* in Rodgers and Hammerstein's *Carousel*. The change of name was by no means the most important difference: the former was more "serious" than the latter, who is flirtatious and a kind of soubrette. Her eventual husband in the play is Wolf Beifeld ("Mr. Snow" in the musical), an ambitious and humorless man. "Mr. Snow," the former Beifeld, is the object of considerable humor in the musical, but with the realization of his ambitions, his marriage to Carrie and being the father of a family, he becomes pompous and bigoted.

The Most Happy Fella/They Knew What They Wanted

This musical by Frank Loesser is based on the play by Sidney Howard. The principal character-alteration in the musical concerns the heroine *Amy*. In the play she is described as "not more than 22 or 23, but she seems older." Her look is, to be sure, "a little tired." She seems bored, a woman of the world who married Tony solely because of the security that such a marriage will give her. At the end of Act I, after discovering that Tony is "old," she says:

No. I ain't going. Why should I go? I like the country. This place suits me all right. It's just what I was looking for. I'm here and I might as well stick. [Etc.]

This speech is a calculated, mercenary decision.

In the musical, the same character, *Rosabella*, sings:

> Somebody, somewhere—
> Wants me and needs me—
> And that's very wonderful to know!

This is feeling without calculation.

But in the musical, at the position that corresponds with the play's Act I ending, Rosabella, having been shocked at identifying Tony, can only say/sing "He's an old man" a number of times.

In addition to the character-change in the heroine, Loesser

79

added three functional people who were not in the original play:

Cleo, a waitress who works with Rosabella in Scene I, is later brought to Tony's ranch to work, but she is introduced especially to provide companionship to Rosabella;

Herman, a ranchhand who becomes Cleo's opposite number, and;

Marie, Tony's dark-souled sister who accentuates Tony's insecurity, the very quality that leads to the unnecessarily complex central situation.

West Side Story/Romeo and Juliet

Jerome Robbins' "concept," based on Shakespeare's *Romeo and Juliet,* was written by Arthur Laurents. Here, the character differences and amalgamations are functional and serve well the change from Verona of about the sixteenth century to New York City at the present time.

Anita, the girlfriend of Bernardo, friend and confidante of the heroine Maria, replaces Shakespeare's *Nurse,* one of whose chief functions is being "listener" and advisor to Juliet. In Shakespeare's play there are twenty-four scenes, but Romeo and Juliet speak to each other in only *four!* However, each character is kept very much alive through each one's references to the other in scenes with other characters. Romeo, for example, speaks of Juliet to Friar Laurence and Mercutio, while Juliet confides in the Nurse.

In *West Side Story,* Maria (Juliet) converses with Tony (Romeo) in seven scenes out of fifteen.

Creating *Bernardo,* Laurents has used Shakespeare's Tybalt, Juliet's cousin, who, having slain Romeo's friend Mercutio, is in turn slain by Romeo. In *West Side Story,* Bernardo is Maria's brother, not cousin, and he is given additional emotional importance *because* he is both Maria's *brother* (slain by Tony, her lover) and Anita's lover.

Doc is Friar Laurence.

Schrank and Krupke, police officers, were originally the Prince of Verona, keeper of the peace.

Chino is Paris, Juliet's fiancé.

Riff is Mercutio, Romeo's friend.

The parents—Montagues and Capulets—have been eliminated in *West Side Story,* but they exist in a different form as the rival gangs—the Jets and the Sharks.

The King and I/Anna and the King of Siam

In Anna Leonowen's original "diary" on which *The King and I* is based, the king is depicted unrelievedly as ruthless, cruel, unattractive, and altogether unreasonable. In the Rodgers and Hammerstein libretto, while he is cruel on at least one occasion, he is endowed with brighter aspects. He has many human facets, is obliquely romantic and likeable despite observable qualities to the contrary. Perhaps one cause of his likeableness is his childish helplessness and his dependency on "Mrs. Anna."

These examples of character alterations should demonstrate the *kinds* of things that help musical shows to achieve their goals—the translation from spoken drama to the lyric, singing theatre.

Many of these changes contribute to the creation of a sub-plot, which I feel is essential to all musicals. One thin (and in a musical) sketchy plot line is insufficient to carry the evening. The show needs relief and contrasts, as does the audience. By "relief," I do not refer to the old "comedy relief," because evolution has taken care of that. In the older shows—it is clearest in *Brigadoon* (1947)—there are the primary romantic pair (in about their late twenties), the comedy pair (same age and a hangover from earlier operetta), and a third set (very young) with a third person—a jilted suitor—to heighten the conflict and suspense. In newer shows, the principal pair, being more three-dimensional, are also given much of the comedy material:

> Mrs. Anna and the king *(The King and I)*
> Nellie Forbush *(South Pacific)*
> Tevya and his wife *(Fiddler on the Roof)*
> Professor Higgins and Eliza *(My Fair Lady)*
> Fredrik and Desirée *(A Little Night Music)*

Now let us compare some scene-by-scene synopses of musicals with their original source material.

Green Grow the Lilacs	*Oklahoma!*
PLAY	MUSICAL
Scene 1—The (Laurey) Williams farmhouse. (This is a living room interior.)	*Act I, Scene 1*—The front of Laurey's farmhouse. (This is out of doors.)
Scene 2—The same, showing Laurey's bedroom. (The material in this scene is included in the musical's first scene.)	
Scene 3—The same, showing the smokehouse.	*Scene 2*—The smokehouse.
	Scene 3—A grove on Laurey's farm. (This scene is an invention of the adapter. It leads into Laurey's dream ballet, which ends in Jud's awakening her and taking her to the social.)

Intermission	Intermission
	Act II, Scene 1—The Skidmore Ranch.
	(This is a new scene in which Will Parker is duped into getting back enough money from the all-too-willing Peddler to be able to marry Ado Annie. Also (and more importantly) there is an auction of picnic baskets, and Jud almost outbids Curly, who has had to sell horse and gun in order to win. Bad feeling between them is expressed.)
Scene 4—The porch of Old Man Peck's house. (The party is in full swing. Laurey has her confrontation with Jeeter, discharges him, and decides to marry Curly.)	*Scene 2*—Skidmore's kitchen porch. (Jud dances on with Laurey. She has the confrontation scene with him and discharges him. She is eager to marry Curly.)
Scene 5—The hay-field back of Williams's house, a month later.	*Scene 3*—Back of Laurey's house. (The setting is the same in both. The wedding of Laurey and Curly is over, and their friends give them a "shivaree"—a customary folk celebration—which is a prankish annoyance to the couple. Here, as in the play, Jud enters, starts an argument and, in a fight with Curly, falls on his own knife. In the musical Aunt Eller amusingly arranges Curly's trial on the spot, and the
Scene 6—The living room of the Williams house three nights later. (Ado Annie and Aunt Eller discuss Curly's trial scheduled for next day. Laurey is worried. Curly enters, having broken out of jail. He is pursued by a crowd of men who mean to return him to jail. Aunt Eller talks them into letting	

Curly spend the night with
his bride.)

show ends with the happy
couple leaving on their
honeymoon.)

Liliom

Prologue—An amusement park
on the outskirts of Budapest.

Scene 1—A lonely place in the
park.

Scene 2—The photographic
studio of the Hollunders.

Scene 3—Same as *Scene 2*.

Scene 4—A railroad
embankment outside
the city.

Scene 5—Same as *Scene 2*.

Scene 6—A courtroom in the
Beyond.

Scene 7—Julie's garden.
Sixteen years later.

Carousel

Prologue—An amusement park
on the New England coast.
May.

Act I, Scene 1—A tree-lined
path along the shore. A few
minutes later.

Scene 2—Nettie Fowler's spa
on the ocean front. June.

Act II, Scene 1—On an island
across the bay, that night.

Scene 2—Mainland waterfront,
an hour later.

Scene 3—Up there.

Scene 4—Down here. On a
beach, fifteen years later.

Scene 5—Outside Julie's
cottage.

Scene 6—Outside a
schoolhouse, same day.

Prologue—similar in both.

Act I, Scene 1—similar in both.

Scene 2—is somewhat similar in both versions: the Hollunders of the play become "Nettie Fowler" in *Carousel*. The difference in mood between play and musical is great. In the play, much attention is given to accounts of Liliom's beating of Julie, which is only mentioned in the musical.

Act II, Scene 1 (musical) provides a musical opening for Act II, a comedy scene between Carrie and Jigger, and the departure of Billy and Jigger to stage the holdup.

Scene 5 (play) contains the death of Liliom (he has been brought home to die) and his march to "heaven." All of this happens in Act II, Scene 2, in the musical, except for the fact that Billy dies almost at once where he has stabbed himself.

Scene 6 (play) and Act II, Scene 3 (musical), are essentially the same—the action is similar but the spirit and ambience are nearly antithetical. In the play, the judgment and sentencing of Liliom are serious and harsh. The musical scene is charming and light.

Act II, Scene 4 (musical) contains the Beach Ballet. This purports to show Billy's daughter, and how she is snubbed because of Billy's shady life and suicide.

Scene 7 (play) is very much like Act II, Scene 5, of the musical, but the scene ends the play with Billy's exit to heaven. Act II, Scene 6, of the musical provides an opportunity for Billy to do his "good deeds" (i.e., he tells Julie that he loves her, and tells his daughter that she does not have to suffer for his misdeeds). It also provides for an "up" musical ending.

Romeo and Juliet	*West Side Story*
ACT ONE	ACT ONE
1. *A Public Place.*	1. *The Street.*
Establishes warring factions. (Montagues/Romeo's family/and Capulets/	Establishes warring factions. (The Jets/Tony's group/and the Sharks/Maria's brother's.)

Juliet's.) Prince of Verona intercedes in a street fight and orders the Capulets to go with him, leaving the Montagues to see him later. The Montegues speak of Romeo. Where is he and why is he sad? He enters. He is in love.

Officer Krupke and a plain-clothesman Shrank intercede and order the Sharks away. Officers exit. There will be a "rumble." The Jets need Tony, who has not been with them lately. Riff will go to reenlist him.

2. *A Street.*

Capulet will give a party. Gives guest list to servant who cannot read. Paris asks Capulet for Juliet's hand. Servant encounters Romeo (a stranger) and asks him to read list. Find's it's Capulet's party and Romeo's love, Rosalin, will attend. Romeo decides to attend also: "I'll go along . . . to rejoice in splendour of mine own."

2. *A Backyard.*

Riff (Mercutio) tries to persuade Tony to rejoin the Jets. Tony finally agrees to join them at the dance that evening. He is obsessed with the feeling ". . . there's a miracle due, Gonna come true, Coming to me!"

3. *A Room in Capulet's House.*

Lady Capulet tells Juliet of Paris's suit, asks her to consider it.

3. *A Bridal Shop.*

Maria with Anita (functions much as the Nurse). Latter is fitting the excited Maria in a dress for tonight and the dance. We meet Bernardo (Tybalt). For Maria it is important that she have a wonderful time at her first dance.

4. *A Street.*

Romeo and Mercutio en route for Capulet's party. Romeo has premonitions of death.

86

5. *Capulet's Party.*

Romeo and friends wearing masks. Romeo sees and is instantly in love with Juliet. Tybalt (Juliet's beloved cousin) recognizes Romeo and wants to fight but Capulet forbids it. Tybalt exits. Juliet is smitten with Romeo, who says "Is she a Capulet? O dear account! My life is in my foe's debt."

4. *The Gym.*

Members of the rival gangs are present with their girlfriends. A "social director" (Capulet) tries to draw them together: "You form two circles: boys on the outside, girls on the inside. . . . When the music stops, each boy dances with whichever girl is opposite." Tony and Maria meet and are instantly in love. Bernardo (Tybalt) observes and berates both, ordering Maria to go home with Chino (Paris). The Jets and Sharks will meet in half an hour at Doc's Drugstore (Tony works there) for a "council of war." Tony is thinking only of Maria.

ACT TWO

1. *A Lane by the Wall of Capulet's Orchard.*

Romeo enters Capulet's orchard. Mercutio and Benvolio realize that he has climbed the wall into the orchard.

2. *Capulet's Orchard.* (Balcony Scene)

Romeo and Juliet, with interruptions by the Nurse. Romeo arranges to send for Juliet next day to be married.

5. *A Back Alley.*

Tony has love scene from street: Maria above on fire escape. Mother's voice interrupts from time to time. Tony agrees to meet Maria next afternoon: he will come to

87

3. *Friar Laurence's Cell.*

Romeo tells of his love for
Juliet to Friar Laurence,
who will marry him.
Friar Laurence thinks the
wedding might heal the rift
between the two families.

4. *Street Scene.*

Mercutio says Romeo has a
letter awaiting him from
Tybalt. The Nurse comes.
Romeo arranges with her to
bring Juliet in the afternoon
to Friar Laurence's cell.

5. *Capulet's Orchard.*

Juliet impatiently awaits
return of Nurse, who finally
arrives and tells her of the
wedding plans.

6. *Friar Laurence's Cell.*

Romeo and Friar Laurence
await arrival of Juliet. After
she joins them they exit
for the wedding.
Friar Laurence: "Come, come
with me, and we will make
short work; . . ."

bridal shop—back door—at
sundown. Bernardo and Anita
enter (Tony has just gone).
Anita is opposed to Bernardo's
warring attitude.

6. *The Drugstore.*

The Jets are edgily awaiting
arrival of Bernardo for the
"council of war." Bernardo
arrives and is taunted. Tony
bursts in happily, understands
what the meeting is about. He
shames both sides into an
agreement that one man
(the best) of each will have a
fair fight without weapons.
Lieutenant Schrank enters and
threatens all of them if
they fight. After he leaves,
Tony, left with Doc, says how
much in love he is.

7. *The Bridal Shop.*

Anita is about to leave when
Tony arrives. Anita doesn't
object to his seeing Maria, but
she is worried. After she
leaves them, Maria begs Tony
to stop the rumble and he
promises that he will. There

follows a wedding ceremony
(minus a minister).
"One hand, one heart—
Even death won't part us
now."

8. *The Neighborhood.*

A musical scene in which all
of the characters appear, but
separately and "abstractly."
All are waiting expectantly for
the night, but for very
different reasons.

ACT THREE

1. *Verona. A Public Place.*

Mercutio and Benvolio speak
of avoiding the Capulets—not
wanting to fight, but when
Tybalt enters, Mercutio picks
a quarrel with him. Romeo
enters and tries to dismiss
Tybalt's taunts. Mercutio
draws his sword. Romeo
tries to prevent the duel, but
it occurs and Mercutio is
slain. Romeo takes up the
fight and Tybalt is slain.
Romeo flees. The Prince
arrives, outraged, and
sentences Romeo to exile

9. *Under the Highway.*

The gangs are waiting to
begin the rumble. As Ber-
nardo and Diesel move to
fight, Tony enters and stops
them. He is taunted from both
sides. Little by little he is
insufferably angered. General
fighting breaks out. Bernardo,
then Riff, reach for their
knives. Tony persists in trying
to stop them. Bernardo
stabs Riff. Tony grabs Riff's
knife and stabs Bernardo. A
free-for-all has broken out.
Police whistles sound.
Everyone disappears quickly,
leaving a stunned Tony
standing over the bodies of
Riff and Bernardo, crying out
"Maria!"

ACT TWO

2. *Capulet's Orchard.*

Nurse tells Juliet of Tybalt's death (Juliet loved her cousin Tybalt) and of Romeo's banishment. Juliet sends Nurse to Friar Laurence's cell to find Romeo.

3. *Friar Laurence's Cell.*

Romeo hears of his exile. Nurse enters, and Romeo says he will come to Juliet.

4. *Capulet's House.*

Disturbances over Tybalt's death. Paris is promised marriage with Juliet on Thursday. (This is Monday.)

1. *A Bedroom.*

Maria with her girlfriends. She is happy. There will be no rumble. The girls exit as Chino enters from the rumble. He tells Maria that Tony killed Bernardo, and leaves, Maria kneels at prayer when Tony enters from the fire escape. Maria is bitter as Tony recounts Riff's death, then Bernardo's. Tont will give himself up to the Police. Maria relents and forbids. Tony will take Maria away: "Suddenly they are in a world of space and air and sun." Others join them "making a world that Tony and Maria want to be in, belong to, share their love with." Jets and Sharks are joined together.

2. *Another Alley.*

The Jets. Where is Tony? Officer Krupke enters, wanting to question them. They elude him and regroup. (Comedy song.) All decide to look for Tony, fearing that Chino will kill him.

5. Romeo has spent the night with Juliet,

3. *The Bedroom.*

Maria and Tony are asleep. There is knocking at the door.

who later is told of
her forthcoming
marriage to Paris.

It is Anita. Tony says he will
go to the drugstore to hide out
and climbs out on the fire
escape. Anita enters and
comprehends the situation.
She is savage to Maria, but, in
the end, turns to help her.
(Together):

"When love comes so strong,
There is no right or wrong,
Your love is your life!"

Shrank comes to question
Maria, who asks Anita to go to
the drugstore (she says she has
a headache) to tell Doc to hold
the medicine there until she
can come for it herself.

ACT FOUR

1. *Friar Laurence's Cell.*

Friar Laurence gives Juliet a
vial. If she drinks the contents
the night before her projected
marriage to Paris, it will make
her appear dead. Paris also
comes to Friar Laurence's cell
and speaks to Juliet of their
marriage.

2. *Capulet's House.*

Juliet returns, tells her parents
she consents to the marriage
with Paris.

3. *Juliet's Chamber.*

Juliet drinks potion.

4. *Capulet's House.*

Marriage preparations.
"To waken Juliet."

5. *Juliet's Chamber.*

Nurse discovers "dead" Juliet.
(Peter and musicians have
comedy scene.)
(This comedy scene
corresponds with *West Side
Story*, Act Two, Scene 2, song,
"Gee, Officer Krupke.")

ACT FIVE

1. *Mantua—a Street.*

Banished Romeo. His servant
Balthazar tells of Juliet's
"death," and Romeo resolves
to go to Juliet's tomb and
brings poison for suicide.

2. *Friar Laurence's Cell.*

Friar John returns with a
letter that Friar Laurence
had written Romeo about
Juliet. Friar John had not been
able to deliver it.

4. *The Drugstore.*

The Jets are standing by.
Tony is hiding out in the
basement. Anita comes to deliver Maria's message. The
boys mistrust and taunt her
savagely. She becomes angry
and blurts out, "Tell the
murderer Maria's never going
to meet him! Tell him Chino
found out and—shot her!"

5. *The Cellar.*

Doc tells Tony what Anita has
said. Tony rushes out in the
darkness yelling "Chino?

Chino, come and get me, too, Chino."

3. *A Churchyard.*

Paris arrives to keep guard at Juliet's tomb. Romeo enters with Balthazar. Paris challenges Romeo and is killed. Romeo takes poison and dies. Juliet wakens, discovers Romeo, and stabs herself. The warring houses (Capulets and Montagues) renounce their enmity.

6. *The Street.*

Tony is still yelling for Chino. He sees Maria. As he runs toward her, Chino appears and shoots him. Members of both gangs appear and lift up Tony's body as they exit.

Pygmalion

Act I—Outside Covent Garden.

Act II—Next day. Higgins' laboratory on Wimpole Street.

Act III—Mrs. Higgins' at-home day.

My Fair Lady

Act I, Scene 1—Outside Covent Garden.

Scene 2—Tenement section, Tottenham Court Road, immediately following.

Scene 3—Higgins' study. The following morning.

Scene 4—Tenement section. Three days later.

Scene 5—Higgins' study. Later that day.

Scene 6—Near the race meeting, Ascot. A July afternoon.

Scene 7—Inside a club tent, Ascot. Immediately following.

Scene 8—Outside Higgins'
house, Wimpole Street.
Later that afternoon.

Scene 9—Higgins' study. Six
weeks later.

Scene 10—The promenade
outside the ballroom of the
embassy.

Scene 11—The embassy
ballroom.

Act IV—The Wimpole Street
laboratory. Midnight.

Act II, Scene 1—Higgins' study.
3 A.M. the following morning.

Scene 2—Outside Higgins'
house.
Immediately following.

Scene 3—Covent Garden. The
flower market.

Scene 4—The upstairs hall of
Higgins' house.

Act V—Mrs. Higgins'
drawing room.

Scene 5—The conservatory of
Mrs. Higgins' house.

Scene 6—Outside of Higgins'
house.

Scene 7—Higgins' study.
Immediately following.

Eliza's father, Alfred P. Doolittle, is introduced in Act II in
the play, when he demands payment for Eliza's "services." In
the musical, he is introduced in Act I, Scene 2, and encountered again in Scene 4, both inserted scenes, after which he
determines to go to Higgins; and in Scene 5, in Higgins' study,
he demands the money.

Act III (play) and Act I, Scenes 6 and 7 (musical), despite the differences in locale, serve the same purpose—introducing Eliza into society for the first time and bringing her together with Freddie.

Act I, Scene 8 (musical), allows Freddie to sing a love song to Eliza, although she is not present.

In Act I, Scene 9 (musical), everyone at Higgins' house is dressed for the ball, and there is great apprehension.

Act I, Scenes 10 and 11 (musical), *show* the presentation of Eliza, and the act ends begging the question of Eliza's success.

Act IV (play) occurs in Act II, Scenes 1 and 2, of the musical.

Act II, Scene 3 (musical), is a partially "invented" scene. Eliza reminisces about her past and encounters her now-successful father, who is about to be married. This latter action takes place in Mrs. Higgins' drawing room in Act V of the play.

Act II, Scene 4 (musical), is an "invented" scene. Higgins, Pickering, and Mrs. Pearce are frantically trying to account for Eliza's departure and to locate her.

The play ends in Act V. In the musical, two consecutive scenes (6 and 7) in Act II develop Higgins' need for Eliza and her eventual return. The play ends with "She's going to marry Freddie." The musical *suggests* an "understanding" between Higgins and Eliza, who has returned to him.

South Pacific, not having been based on a play but on several short stories—*Tales of the South Pacific*, by James A. Michener—illustrates a different approach to libretto adaptation. The characters and the situations were selected from nineteen short stories that ranged in length from three to sixty-four printed pages. The general background of the show is drawn, in a very loose sense, from *all* of the tales, but three specific ones yielded the principal characters and the particular situations.

"Our Heroine" occupies twenty-seven pages in the collection. It tells briefly of the romance between Nurse Nellie Forbush and the French plantation owner, Emile de Becque. All of it takes place in a single evening.

"Fo' Dolla" (sixty-four pages) concerns Bloody Mary, 1st Lt. Joe Cable, Bali-ha'i, and Mary's daughter Liat. The romance between the two young people is developed. Mary wants Cable to marry Liat, but considering his position in Philadelphia Main Line society, he is unable to consider marriage with this lovely native girl. At the end of the tale, Lieutenant Cable is transferred to another part of the island.

A third story, "A Boar's Tooth" (fewer than twenty pages), pictures Luther Billis, the "Big Dealer."

The six characters depicted in the three separate tales never spill over into other tales.

Roughly, Hammerstein and Joshua Logan used "Our Heroine" (Nellie and Emile) as the outside framework for the entire libretto. Nellie and Emile were made to be the heroine and the hero, and their romance was what we cared about chiefly. Their schism neatly divided the libretto into two parts. They invented Lieutenant Cable's assignment (spying on Japanese shipping from another island) and Emile's decision to lead him where he had to go (because Nellie had refused to marry him). Emile, in absentia, is kept alive in the show in Act II through his daily radio reports, which Nellie awaits with growing anxiety. During this invented mission, Cable dies, a device that prevents his becoming a heel in refusing to marry Liat.

Luther Billis, who deals in services (laundry) and souvenirs, became a kind of comedic opposite to Bloody Mary, who was similarly engaged. The young romantic tale (Liat and Cable) was encased in the Nellie-Emile framework. Emile's safe return to a chastened Nellie provides a happy (and satisfying) ending to the musical.

The meshing of situations and characters culled from three different stories into a single unit becomes a model, workable libretto.

The best musicals of the past have had somewhat longer first acts than second acts. There are no rules about this, but some first acts contain ten to twelve scenes. The second acts contain five or six. Some of the locales are repeated. A newer practice in some musicals has been to present the entire show in a single act, without interruption (examples: *Pippin, A Chorus Line, Man of La Mancha*). The writer does not have to concern himself with matters involving scenery, as an experienced designer will know many ways—depending upon the style of the production—to design or suggest changes of scenery. What the librettist or synopsist must be concerned with, however, are costumes, to the extent that performers be given sufficient time to change from, let us say, a tennis outfit to evening clothes. This is at least one reason for not having performers follow themselves from one scene to another.

Shakespeare is a perfect model for this avoidance. One character concludes a scene (*The Comedy of Errors,* Act II, Scene 2) with:

> I'll to the mart, and there for Dromio stay.
> If any ship put out, then straight away.

You may be certain that the very next scene is *not* the mart, but a different place with a different set of characters. In this way, sets of characters or combinations of people alternate with one another.

This subject of scenes (or "cells") brings one to another

important point, amply illustrated by Shakespeare. In multi-scene shows (musicals and plays of many classic writers) each scene must conclude with two things that happen simultaneously: by its content (not by a blackout or the dropping of a curtain) we must know that the scene has ended (as with an exclamation point), and at the same time an index finger must point ahead to further action. In other words, no scene should be allowed merely to fade away, and no scene should stop without giving the audience a definite promise of future action: it must be going somewhere.

This brings up the question of time-space. The action of *West Side Story* covers a period of about one day, giving it a feeling of urgency. I believe all musicals should occupy a tightly knit time span.

In his recent *Memoirs*, Tennessee Williams, in speaking of his play *Cat on a Hot Tin Roof*, says: ". . . its running time is exactly the time of its action, meaning that one act, timewise, follows directly upon the other . . ." and he favors this tightness.

The question of being "faithful" to the original is generally irrelevant. The answer rests with what the adaptors (including composer and lyricist) are able to accomplish in their own way, with whatever serves their own purposes best.

Despite cuts and additions, *My Fair Lady* is truly a musicalization of *Pygmalion*, but there are few other examples of translation from one media to another that—for a variety of reasons—have been accomplished so directly.

To point to a recent unfortunate adaptation (not a musical), consider Neil Simon's comedy, *God's Favorite*, which was a setting—contemporary in time and place—of the Book of Job. Anyone undertaking such an ambitious project has to consider carefully several major problems. First, what special something has *this* author to add to the original? What comment of his own does he intend to make? Will he use this material to arrive at a different conclusion? (All of this is part of one question.)

Second, if he plans to make it contemporary *and* a comedy, he must necessarily abandon the glorious poetry of the original or of the King James version of the Bible which we know so well. In that case, what will he replace it with?

Neither question was answered satisfactorily. The beautiful poetry was replaced with humorous one-liners of the kind Simon is famous for. This already shortchanges the audience. To answer the first question, Simon had no comment of his own, no new conclusion to arrive at, nothing to add. And so the result was dissatisfying and Simon's choice of the Book of Job for "rewriting" seemed wasteful.

On the other hand, the use of *Romeo and Juliet* as a basis for *West Side Story* was fortuitous. The writers took the *universality* of the original and the two principal characters and translated them into our own time and place—making the project their own. They even went one step further: having converted the two warring families into two contemporary warring gangs, Laurents then showed us how pathetically they themselves were also the victims of society. Although they *appeared* to cause the tragedy, they were also the victims. In a sense, Shakespeare had the same conclusion in mind.

Something similar came out of *Fiddler on the Roof*, which was based on stories of Sholom Aleichem. The tale was set around the turn of this century in Poland and concerned itself with a community of Jews who lived by their traditions and were destroyed as families, but the older people were also led onward to an uncertain future by their strong beliefs. That is the tale. But what transcended it and made it so relevant here and now and everywhere in the world was its basic *theme*, which was the generation gap and its effect on one family—the children who were pulling away and the parents who had to live on with, and because of, their beliefs.

When Rodgers and Hammerstein undertook the musicalization of Molnár's *Liliom* and changed the locale and the time to the coast of New England about 1873, they destroyed one of that play's most memorable qualities: the atmosphere of Budapest in 1919. It was a brave thing to have undertaken, but Rodgers and Hammerstein were the winners, for they endowed *Carousel* with songs that transcended much of the original play and they created an entirely new atmosphere that satisfactorily replaces the one they destroyed.

Loesser made a vibrant *Most Happy Fella* out of a creaky *They Knew What They Wanted. Oklahoma!* rescued *Green Grow the Lilacs* from obscurity. *Cabaret* revived *I Am a Camera. The King and I* saved *Anna and the King of Siam* from oblivion. And there are many other examples. While the songs had a great deal to do with these successful transplants, the complete takeover of the original material, making it the adaptor's very own, was in every case crucial. Had this not happened, had only halfway measures been taken, the musical projects would have been doomed.

One of the reasons the ending of a play or musical is seldom a surprise is that the playwright or librettist has told or indicated *everything* that must happen during the show's progress. In *1776*, there is a calendar on the wall of the Continental Congress' meeting place. Each day, one date is peeled off and we are fast approaching July 4 (1776). The audience *knows* that the Declaration of Independence was signed on July 4, yet in 1776 on July 3, we cannot see how such a thing could possibly take place the next day since the opposing parties seem farther apart than ever. The calendar device serves to reinforce the audience's anxiety because *it* has previous knowledge while the characters in the show do not know what will happen.

In *Othello,* we know the truth about Iago and Desdemona: his motivation and her complete innocence. Othello knows neither and he therefore becomes Iago's pawn. If we could only tell him . . . but then there would be no play, which is based dramatically on his *not* knowing.

In *The Comedy of Errors,* two sets of twins are involved in a dizzying series of mischances. The audience knows clearly which Antipholus and which Dromio is which. The characters who confuse them are innocent of the very certainties that we are given. We follow the action, while the complex plot is based on the befuddlement of everyone in it. Further, Shakespeare, at the outset of his play, introduces the father of the twins—both named Antipholus—who is being sentenced to death and given a day to raise sufficient money for his own ransom. He thinks he has lost his two sons and their two twin servants. This death sentence (locating the sons would clear up the charges against the father) motivates the ensuing action.

There are two kinds of plays or novels that, in my opinion, are doomed to fail if musicalization is attempted. The first is the mystery story. I feel it is impossible (or, at the very least, extremely difficult) to make this work because one of the most common devices in all mystery tales is the use of "red herrings"—casting doubt and suspicion on innocent characters in order to heighten the suspense, confuse the reader, and prolong the novel. If this were done in a musical, there would be *no* character with whom an audience could wholly empathize; further, the audience would be uncertain as to the character for whom it should "root." The fabric of a mystery story is, of necessity, complex. There are numerous plots, counterplots, and subplots, and keeping track of them would be even more difficult if music were added. Finally, the chief emotion in such tales is fear coupled with uncertainty. Love is suspect, as is hate. What the author builds toward is simply the very end: whodunit? Everything leading to that one *raison d'être* is decorative, either preventing the reader (audience) from guessing the outcome, or relating more or less directly to it. In a musical, while the ending must satisfy (it is what the librettist *makes* the audience want), it need not be—and seldom is—a surprise. All the rest that is to be sung about is what must satisfy or fail.

The other kind of play that in my opinion is difficult, if not impossible, to musicalize is the *farce.* The reader may point to the Stephen Sondheim–Burt Shevelove *A Funny Thing Happened on the Way to the Forum,* based on an old farce by the Roman playwright Plautus. Perhaps this is the exception that proves the rule. Perhaps it works as a musical because despite its complexities it is basically about a slave who wants his freedom above everything else. Romance, comic situation on top of comic situation, confusion of identities, and much, much more are only contributing factors to the main idea. Besides, all the characters are easily related to: the overbearing wife, the sex-starved husband, the beautiful-but-dumb girl-next-door, the "nice" boy, and the rest. How familiar they are to everyone. I am not suggesting that *A Funny Thing Happened on the Way to the Forum* is simpleminded, but I am attempting to say that the *familiarity* of these people to us is helpful in simplifying much of the exposition.

However, if you read the delightful farces ("chases") of Feydeau, Labiche, and others, you will see that they are breathless. In a sense, they are frantic ballets without music—complex, fabricated, and very, very funny. The characters are not—at least today—familiar to us. I think we care a great deal about the dizzying situations and not very much about the people. The erring wife means as much to us as the cuckolded husband.

Again I do not intend any of this as criticism, but I feel

strongly that the introduction of songs to any of these farces is going to stop the speedy action which is at the root of the fun.

Another caution to be taken is in regard to the employment of material for a musical (for a play also) based on history or biography. True, both have been used successfully by many playwrights, as in the case of the musical, *1776*, in which history was employed to advantage. However, the dialogue was not reproduced from an ancient tape recorder!

Most people think of history and biography in terms of accuracy, but accuracy should be the least of the worries of either the playwright or the librettist. What creative people need to do in both cases is to *create*. (Shakespeare did.) If the book-writer has nothing of his own to add, nothing that he himself has dreamed up, what is the point of his trying to fashion a stage piece? Facts, data, historical truths are for readers of biography, scholars, and students. Alone, these lack the magic that the stage requires. To illustrate: the best play about Queen Elizabeth I and Mary, Queen of Scots is the one by the German poet-playwright Friedrich von Schiller called *Mary Stuart*. The excitement that this play generates comes from the author's imagination: he stages a confrontation between the two queens at the center of the play, and all that precedes and follows is related to the planning and results of that clash. Now, the historical truth is that these two ladies *never met at all!* But why should an audience care whether this is true or not? The only thing we do care about is whether or not the play interests and excites or bores us. All other theatre treatments I have ever seen or read about either or both queens have been accurate, and accuracy alone, as I said earlier, is dry bones on the stage.

If a librettist wants to base a work for the stage on either history or biography, he must begin with one or more factual characters in a more-or-less general situation and then he must throw away the books he has read, *dream*, and utilize the basic material as his dreams dictate.

Last, I am well aware that talented musical-theatre writers are painstakingly grasping for new forms, and I greatly admire their efforts, their sincerity, and often their considerable talents. However, here I should like to be specific in treating one particular show that was packed with talent and that, in my opinion, did not work: *Pacific Overtures*—music and lyrics by Stephen Sondheim, based on a book by John Weidman, staged and produced by Harold Prince, with sets by Boris Aronson and costumes by Florence Klotz.

Let us dispose of the best contributions first. The majority of Sondheim's songs are exquisite and funny. Aronson's sets are breathtakingly beautiful and tasteful. Florence Klotz's costumes are likewise incredibly effective. The lovely orchestrations of Jonathan Tunick must also be added to the credit side, as must be Harold Prince's staging, which was always interesting. Most of all one must deeply admire the courage and drive that these artists expended in a sincere effort to explore a new form.

I believe I know some of the reasons for the show's failure, and all of them, in my opinion, are attributable to the eschewing of basic principles that must exist in every theatre work, irrespective of what might appear on the surface as "new."

At first, for me there was a trace of feeling in the first quarter of an hour that I think results from the establishment of characters with whom we can empathize. The empathy, however, is short-lived because the authors have gone in for an enormously long time span. Thus, the characters we have first met and who we are prepared to follow through their own experiences and developments are phased out early in a show that covers 130-odd years. There are, therefore, no continuing central characters. The show is about the first opening up of isolated Japan by Commodore Perry and the subsequent widening of Japan's relations with all other countries of the world.

Now, these are *facts* of history; but I do not think that facts are enough to satisfy theatre audiences. Indeed, much of the show is musically and visually entertaining, but the thread running through it is icy cold, and we are left with nothing about which we can care. Although the actors playing the original characters who initially interested us continue on throughout the show as other characters, it is not the same thing. We do not *care* about the actors but about the people they represented.

Then, too, despite the fact that the production employs an excellent narrator who from time to time assumes roles within the play, and despite the fact that *Pacific Overtures* allegedly tells the story of United States–Japanese relations between Commodore Perry's arrival in Japan and the present, time elapses without any mention of Pearl Harbor or Hiroshima and Nagasaki. One narrative sentence would have sufficed. These world-shaking events had catastrophic effects on our relationship with Japan and resulted in hitherto unheard-of devastation. Yet there is not a single allusion in the show to any of this havoc.

Either *Pacific Overtures* is a history (it is) or it is an imaginative entertainment (which it only partially is). Most of the entertainment is supplied by the music and lyrics, costumes, magical lights and scenery; but the book, the progress, the theme (is there a theme?) are lost.

My personal objections to the musical contributions are minor in the light of its accomplishments. To be exact, I have two: first is the second act opening, in which emissaries from five countries come to Japan to effect trade agreements. For this, the music imitates five national styles in the most obvious ways, adapting too-familiar clichés to identify each character.

The whole sequence, in my opinion, is far below the level of the enormous gifts of Stephen Sondheim.

The other musical miscalculation occurs because of the use of a nearly all-male cast that is attributed to Kabuki-style theatre; this, in my opinion, is too flimsy an excuse. Who needs to care? There is a scene-song, "Welcome to Kanagawa," utilizing the madam of a whorehouse and four of her "girls." Only at the very start of the number did I feel a sense of amusement. Afterward, I was too easily reminded of similar numbers in the early Thirties—performed at "gay" nightclubs. My opposition to men playing women arose from the fact that it was not new; neither did it belong in the theatre. The "excuse" that was offered was that the show was in the style of the Kabuki. The authentic Kabuki has been accepted everywhere, but suggesting its style and simply borrowing one element from it (its all-male cast) seems unsatisfying to me. It is like taking mayonnaise from a smorgasbord, and claiming that it is indeed smorgasbord.

Sondheim's other songs were brilliant, especially "Chysanthemum Tea" and "A Bowler Hat," which was so theatrical that hearing it on records I missed the visual elements supplied on the the stage. This, I count as a compliment.

Most of all—in recapitulation—was the absence of developing characters to be followed and cared about. I doubt that the musical theatre can ever—in one way or another—depart successfully from such a basic core.

Today, young people especially—more aggressive and with flimsier ties to the past—ask a question to which I have never successfully found the answer: why must musicals be based on adaptations of plays, novels, films, and other existing literary material? This is the same question that has obviously been of considerable concern to Sondheim, who must be praised for his efforts in attempting to find new directions. But for all of his efforts, we are left with marvelous scores to "original" librettos that come off less successfully than the music. *Anyone Can Whistle, Company, Follies,* and *Pacific Overtures* are clear examples of libretto weaknesses. On the other hand, *A Little Night Music,* adapted from Ingmar Bergman's film *Smiles of a Summer Night,* was thoroughly successful.

Perhaps the difference between working with the brand-new idea and an adaptation of a tested one—even a tested one that failed in its original state *(Green Grow the Lilacs* that became *Oklahoma!* is an example) serves the librettist best because it does offer him already-made characters and a serviceable plot line. The employment of these pre-made characters is often subject to change, a matter already discussed (for instance, the addition of the characters Will Parker in *Oklahoma!* and Cleo in *The Most Happy Fella;* and the alteration of the characters Ado Annie in *Oklahoma!,* the king in *The King and I,* and many others). However, something basic existed before the librettist began his work of transformation. He could go *with* it or *against* it. I feel certain that this cannot be the *only* reason for the use of adaptations, but it is surely one of them.

I'm beginning to believe a departure in at least one direction has taken place. I cannot classify *A Chorus Line* as an "original" because all of the many brief tales have been selected and edited from true-life ones, and no one of them spreads over and is developed at length sufficient to cover an entire evening. However, these many different tales have been told completely in lyrics and/or dramatic recitations, and all are held together by a common tie: all of the characters have assembled in one place in order to audition for jobs in the dancing ensemble of a projected musical show.

One show cannot indicate a trend; but more recently we have seen *Comedians,* an interesting play by Trevor Griffiths that employs a similar method. In *Comedians*, a small group of men with different backgrounds and occupations have assembled to learn how to become comedians. In Act I, we learn of the character traits peculiar to each. In Act II, they audition individually in a pub in Manchester for a London theatrical agent. In Act III, we learn the results.

The fact that the characters in both *A Chorus Line* and *Comedians* are brought together in a common purpose, that our attention is held by their individual tales, and that there is in both shows an overall theme but no overall tale, places the two shows in a single new category.

Certainly the invention or the employment of a number of small tales bundled together under one aegis is an easier device to sustain than the one large tale abetted by subplot(s) which requires greater and longer development. Also, in the vignette group, the characters are not alotted overmuch time, so the responsibility of in-depth searching is neither mandatory nor even possible.

Somewhat related to these two shows is *Company*, which employs five couples, one unattached protagonist, and three single girls. Such a broad list of characters, almost equal in size of roles, surrounding the single male "hero" also limits the responsibility of the writer in that no single character has to be developed and, as in the cases of the previously mentioned shows, there is no one ongoing plot.

Finally, the non-musical theatre's best new plays are generally based on themes and are themselves plotless. In such cases, the responsibility of the author is twofold: he must necessarily develop his characters extensively and he must provide interest or entertainment (not to be confused with amusement) throughout. Having no plot means having no predictable outcome. Pinter's *The Birthday Party* is fraught with suspense. His latest play *No Man's Land* is nearly always amusing, often mystifying; but the audience that allows itself to be is fascinated by the characters: who are they, why are they together, where are they going?

I would strongly advise the librettist, at least at this stage of musical-theatre development, against the use of total plotlessness and/or ambiguity. By employing plotlessness, the responsibility to be borne by music and lyrics would be beyond anyone's power to deal with satisfactorily. By attempting the ambiguity which has worked so well in plays by Ionesco, Beckett, Pinter, Storey, Albee, Stoppard, and others, the thinking audience is titillated both during the performance of their plays and long afterward; but if any of these plays were complimented by music, the resultant complexity would be more than anyone could bear. Besides, it is only the *specific* that can be sung about, and ambiguity's stock-in-trade is use of the nonspecific.

The one truth that can be observed in this *avant garde* trend is that it works only when the audience's interest is piqued, when this interest is sustained, and when the audience is made to care about the characters. All this remains the requisite of the good workable libretto.

THE MAKING OF A SYNOPSIS

Let us now take a play that is trivial and dated, *The Moon Is Blue* by F. Hugh Herbert. Produced in 1951, it gave 924 performances. But it could not survive its own time for very long, not only because it was flimsy, but because its leading lady was a "professional virgin"—a condition considered disreputable today. It is inconceivable that the author ever thought of this little four-character play as anything more than a pot-boiler, but it succeeded at the time as a play and as a film, and I think it made a great deal of money.

I recommend it, however, as an ideal basis for an exercise in synopsis-making for musical libretto study. First, there are too few characters—really only three, with a fourth who appears only briefly. A prologue and an epilogue take place in the Observation Tower of the Empire State Building, a glamorous place in the Thirties. However, the body of the three-act play takes place in the apartment of the hero.

As the adaptor will be using this as an exercise—*not* for publication or for production—he should not have to be concerned with obtaining the rights.

Although I will make a synopsis later, I will first point out some facets of this play which can be of some help to the student.

First of all, the telephone was a favorite device in drawing-room comedies of the Twenties and Thirties, and in small-cast plays of the period. Why the telephone? Because, as in the beginning of *No, No, Nanette* when the maid answers the phone, she provides the audience with the names of characters, who they are, where they are, etc. But in *No, No, Nanette* we eventually meet them. In *The Moon Is Blue,* they play offstage parts and we never see them, and in making a viable synopsis we have to employ many other people and must create out of them a subplot, several of which I will suggest.

First, let us consider the people who are seen:

Patty O'Neill, a young unemployed actress

Donald Gresham, a young architect

David Slater, a "fast and loose," wealthy older man

Michael O'Neill, Patty's father—a cop (He appears only briefly in a single scene.)

Now let us list the other people who are mentioned or spoken to on the telephone but never seen:

Cynthia Slater, David's daughter and Don's fiancé

Vicki, Patty's roommate

Mrs. Slater, divorced wife of David

"A young lady" found by Cynthia with David

It is not necessary in this case to "dream" profoundly of other character possibilities. First, all the mentioned ones could be employed. Then it would be likely that Vicki, Patty's roommate, would have a boyfriend; that her father would have a wife; that Cynthia, who seems to have "been around," would have other male friends besides Don. There are endless other possibilities.

As for "opening up the proscenium" (desirable in a musical), Don, as an architect, has an office. Patty and Vicki have living quarters. David has an apartment in the same building with Don. Patty, as an unemployed actress, would visit theatrical offices, possibly take classes, go to a photographer, pose for advertisements, etc. Cynthia, who is frequently telephoning Don, could be met *outside* his apartment—at the neighborhood delicatessen, bar, discotheque, or many other public places, since Don's apartment is presently "occupied."

The one deterrent to updating *The Moon Is Blue* is its leading lady's insistence on preserving her virginity. The locale, I believe, is indigenous to New York City, but it is conceivable that the show could take place in any large city where there is theatrical activity: Chicago, Los Angeles, or several others.

In creating scenes not called for in the play, it is helpful to use (though not necessarily be limited) to ones about which characters only speak. For example, in the prologue, we learn that Don first saw Patty in a drugstore, where she was pricing a lipstick and he was buying rubber bands and a pumice stone. The musical might begin there before the Empire State Building sequence. Or it could start at an audition Patty is giving and then go to Don's office, where he decides to go on an errand (to the drugstore) in order to "stretch his legs." The possibilities of additional characters and locales are inexhaustible.

The synopsis would be written in two acts (the play is in

three) and there would be many scenes. As a synopsis, the language would be telegraphic and the scenes succinctly indicated without lengthy descriptions. The contents of each scene would be described in three or four lines: what happens, who is involved, and what has happened that will lead us ahead. I would *avoid* the incorporation of song titles, as these will tend to obscure the basic structure; also, as titles, they will add nothing to the progress of the synopsis-scenario.

In my opinion, sketching out a first synopsis, especially if it is built around so rapid a situation and such vacuous characters as there are in *The Moon Is Blue*, should be approached in the manner of solving a jigsaw puzzle! Think in a detached way about how you can move the pieces around so that they fit. I would not give this same advice to writers trying to write out a potentially viable libretto. Even so, this kind of work is first of all mechanical. Afterward, the writer fills the structure in with protoplasmic matter.

The following synopsis made from *The Moon Is Blue* as a basis for musicalization is rough and indicates only one of thousands of ways in which this particular assignment can be accomplished.

CAST OF CHARACTERS

Patty O'Neill, a young unemployed actress
Vicki, her roommate, a dancer
Michael O'Neill, Patty's father
Tony Delorso, Vicki's married boyfriend
Donald Gresham, a young architect
David Slater, his boss; older, wealthy, and a playboy
Cynthia Slater, David's daughter, engaged to marry Donald

Act I, Scene 1: A drugstore in the Empire State Building.

Patty and Don at separate counters are pricing merchandise, obviously aware of each other. Patty makes a sudden exit without the lipstick she has priced; Don buys several items quickly, including the lipstick, and goes in pursuit.

Scene 2: An architect's office.

David Slater is talking with his daughter Cynthia, who is upset. Tells her father she tried to spend the night with Don but he put her out of his apartment. David says he will have a talk with Don, and takes Cynthia out to lunch.

Scene 3: Observation Tower, Empire State Building.

Don and Patty become acquainted. He invites her to have a cocktail in his apartment. She asks if he would try to seduce her and he denies such intentions: they will have cocktails and he will take her to the Stork Club for dinner.

Scene 4: Small apartment shared by Patty and Vicki.

Vicki is entertaining her friend Tony, who is eager to go to bed with her (it has become a ritual), but Vicki is disturbed that he won't divorce his wife and marry her. The phone rings; it is Patty, calling to say that she is at Don's apartment and is expecting a call from an agent. Leaves number. Tony asks Vicki out to dinner. As they are about to leave, phone rings. Blackout.

Scene 5: Don's apartment.

Vicki is in Don's bathrobe. They were caught in the rain and her clothes were soaked. Vicki offers to cook dinner, and Don leaves to buy food at the delicatessen. Phone rings, Patty answers and the caller hangs up. Patty calls Vicki and we hear other end of conversation that occurred in Scene 4. Doorbell rings. Patty opens the door to David Slater, who lives upstairs. He is enchanted with her. Conversation regarding Cynthia, about whom Don has already told Patty. Hearing that Patty is unemployed, David offers her $600 he won the night before at gambling—"no strings." Patty finally accepts and is giving him a friendly kiss when Don, laden with groceries, returns. Despite Don's anger, Patty invites David to stay for dinner. Phone rings, Don answers, tells the caller he will meet her at once—not to come there—at Kelly's Bar (neighborhood). Patty and David exit into kitchen.

Scene 6: Kelly's Bar, a little earlier than the preceding scene.

Vicki and Tony are seated at a table, drinking and wrangling over their problem. Cynthia enters alone, goes to the bar, and orders a drink, obviously attracted to Tony and vice versa. Don enters and joins Cynthia. They have an argument. Cynthia accuses him of being interested in another girl. Don admits that there is a girl in his apartment cooking dinner, but Cynthia's father is there also, and Don says he hardly knows the girl. He must leave at once because of dinner, but promises to call Cynthia later.

Scene 7: Don's apartment.

Don returns, and the three are having a turbulent dinner when the doorbell rings. Don goes to the door, Patty's father sees Patty in the bathrobe, knocks out Don, makes Patty put on her clothes, and takes her away, leaving David enjoying the situation and attending Don.

Act II, Scene 1: David's apartment, later that evening.

Cynthia enters with Tony Delorso. Tony has left Vicki, and Cynthia and he are becoming enamored. At the height of this getting together, David returns. Embarrassment. Cynthia says she is finished with Don. Tony says he wants to know Cynthia "seriously." David has only come for some liniment, is not disturbed, and leaves them together, returning to Don.

Scene 2: Patty's apartment.

Patty and her father are having a brawl. She says that nothing was wrong. She is embarrassed. Convinces her father she must go back and apologize, also return money to David. Her father feels he acted too hastily and agrees, provided she promises to come back at once. He will wait for her.

Scene 3: Don's apartment.

David is trying to pacify Don. Doorbell rings. Patty enters. Don is angry because of her father and David. Patty apologizes. Explains about David, returns money. Says she knows Don must hate her, and leaves before Don can find out where she lives, etc.

Scene 4: David's apartment.

Cynthia and Tony are happily together. Tony plans to divorce his wife. The two go out to supper.

Scene 5: Patty's apartment.

Michael O'Neill (Patty's father) is trying to comfort Vicki. They discover they are mutually attracted. Patty returns. Her father explains. Patty goes into her room and leaves happy couple together.

Scene 6: Empire State Building Observatory.

Don is alone, nervous, hoping, but not knowing what to do. Patty enters, hoping to find him. This happens only once in a blue moon.

END

This is not intended as a model, but it does demonstrate what is meant by "opening up the proscenium," adding enough characters to "fatten" the plot, creation of subplot, etc.

It is important, on completion of a synopsis, to determine the number of scenes each character is in so that you may have an explicit idea of how each one is kept alive, especially how many scenes the principals are in, and how widely separated these are.

In the foregoing synopsis:

Patty appears in eight scenes: Act I, Scenes 1, 3, 5, and 7; Act II, Scenes 2, 3, 5, and 6.

Don is in seven scenes: Act I, Scenes 1, 3, 5, 6, and 7; Act II, Scenes 1, 3, and 6.

They appear together in six scenes.

Don is discussed in Act I, Scene 2; Act II, Scenes 1 and 2.

Patty is discussed in Act I, Scene 4.

David appears in Act I, Scenes 2, 5, and 7; Act II, Scenes 1, 2, and 3. *David* is discussed in Act I, Scene 6.

Vicki appears in Act I, Scenes 4 and 6, and Act II, Scene 5.

Cynthia appears in Act I, Scenes 2 and 6; Act II, Scenes 1 and 4. *Cynthia* is talked about in Act I, Scene 5.

Tony appears in Act I, Scenes 4 and 6; Act II, Scenes 1 and 4.

Michael O'Neill appears in Act I, Scene 7; Act II, Scenes 2 and 5. *Michael O'Neill* is spoken of in Act I, Scene 4.

Although this short table is rudimentary, it will nevertheless serve to demonstrate the "keeping alive" of *all* of the characters and the predominance of the two principals.

It also indicates the existence of a main plot (Patty, Don, and David); the relation of Cynthia, Vicki, and Michael to them; and the subplot involving Vicki, Tony, Cynthia, and Michael. The subplot characters do not stand out independent of the principals, but their lives are intertwined with those of the principals; however, the subplot is indeed a complete plot, and there is an implicit "growth" that affects everyone.

No synopsis can adequately explain character, but the writers who must rely on this sort of framework as a basis for creating a musical score are further urged to make character explorations, even by writing—outside of the synopsis—a series of in-depth sketches of each of the roles, examining (creat-

ing) backgrounds for each, earlier histories, ambitions, qualities, etc. By establishing the characters and making a skeletal
synopsis of the action—who, where, when, and what—it is
possible for composers and lyricists to lay the groundwork for
the creation of a musical score.

All of this is subject to subsequent changes, of course, but
it can become enough of a beginning to trigger music and
lyrics. It is my feeling that both composer and lyricist (if they
are two people) should be jointly engaged in creating this
synopsis.

THE PLACEMENT OF SONGS IN A SCENE

One of the most important considerations in writing a musical is *what* to musicalize. When this is not considered carefully
enough, the result is an unconscionable set of stereotypic
songs, usually resulting from the misguided decision to write
songs for which, in parallel situations in nearly every other
show from the beginning of our musical theatre, other songs
were written.

The most common and boring of these occurs when the hero
and heroine are alone on stage and they begin to sing a love
song! Or a man or woman, obviously intended as comedians,
sing a "cute" song. Or the vocal ensemble—merry villagers, in
my vocabulary—are happy, carefree, and tell us who, where,
and when they are, as if the scenery and costumes hadn't
immediately spelled all this out sufficiently.

Like the plays of Shakespeare, musicals are multi-scene
theatre pieces. Each of the many scenes should end forcefully
enough and clearly enough to indicate "The End" to the audience, without the need of a drawn curtain or a blackout. There
are at least three ways to achieve this:

1. Lines can forecast future action as a result of what has immediately preceded this forecast: "We are going someplace" or "We are going to do something." This is most often Shakespeare's method. As an example, I will paraphrase a speech from the end of Act II, Scene 2, in *A Midsummer Night's Dream*. Hermia awakens, startled, from a bad dream:

> Help me, Lysander, help me. . . .
> What, out of hearing gone? . . .
> Either death or you I'll find immediately.

At the end of Act III, Scene 3, in *Twelfth Night*, the following is very much abridged:

Maria (Speaking of Malvolio): "He's in yellow stockings."

Sir Toby: "Come, bring us, bring us where he is."

2. Scenes end with an emphatic exclamation point, also usually pointing ahead to future action. This "exclamation point" may constitute a surprise, shock (serious), or a "joke."

The libretto of *Guys and Dolls* by Jo Swerling and Abe Burrows is filled with these: nearly all the scenes finish explosively, which is usually caused by a surprise that produces laughter. At the end of Act I, Scene 1, for example, the two principal gamblers, Sky Masterson and Nathan Detroit, have played a scene together. Nathan is in dire need of one thousand dollars. He has investigated and learned to his surprise that Mindy's Restaurant sells more of its strudel than its famous cheesecake, and then offers to bet Sky a thousand dollars that this is so. Sky refuses to take the bet and recounts a parable his father had told which, in essence, was: don't make foolish bets because you are going to end up with an earful of cider. After further bantering, Nathan bets Sky that Sky can't take just any "doll" Nathan might point out to Havana tomorrow. Sky accepts this bet, just as the Save-a-Soul Mission Band appears and Nathan designates the leader of the group, a pretty but straitlaced girl, as the subject. Sky yells "Cider!" and there is a blackout.

The situation is amusing and the outcome is awaited with interest. The best musicals contain many examples of this kind.

3. In a musical show, it is often desirable to end a scene with a song, especially if, in any case, a song is to be included in the scene. The presence of a song at the very end is in itself a punctuation, since its ending will help to strengthen the scene's end. Then, too, most good songs elicit applause, which could again coincide with the scene's end.

In *The King and I*, by Rodgers and Hammerstein, four of the six scenes in Act I end with songs; two of the six scenes in Act II have songs at their ends.

In Stephen Sondheim's *A Little Night Music*, five of the seven scenes in Act I and five of the eight scenes in Act II end with songs.

In Frank Loesser's *Guys and Dolls*, out of nine scenes in Act I, four use songs to end scenes, and six out of seven scenes in Act II end with songs.

The above statistics, chosen at random, will indicate that there are no rules. Ending a scene of a musical with a song is only one way, but usually an effective one.

Placement of songs during scenes is both important and difficult: important, because the best songs in the best shows should be functional in addition to being good; difficult, because one must know *what* in the scenes is best chosen for singing and what will not emerge as pure stereotype.

Let us first approach this matter of placement by way of those songs in some of our most successful shows that were suggested directly by dialogue in the original play.

Oklahoma! was adapted by Oscar Hammerstein II from Lynn Riggs' play *Green Grow the Lilacs*. The play opens with

Curly singing a folk-like song, the first line of which is "As I walked out one bright sunny morning." There is actually a suggestion of a topic here, and in the musical this became "Oh, What a Beautiful Morning."

Later in the scene (play), Curly is describing his nonexistent (imaginary) surrey with such images as "with fringe on the top . . . and yeller!" "two white horses," "four fine side-curtains, case of rain," "and isinglass winders." These and many more were integrated into a narrative lyric "The Surrey with the Fringe on Top." The song provides a playful, flirtatious interlude that *indicates* a steady, charming relationship between hero and heroine without any direct reference to it.

Later in the scene, expressing fear of Jeeter (Jud in *Oklahoma!*), Laury says, "I wake up and hear the boards creakin' . . . ." In the musical, Hammerstein uses a similar line to begin Jud's only solo, "Lonely Room," "The floor creaks. . . ."

Scene 3 of the play is in the Smokehouse, most of it between Curly and Jeeter (Jud). In the play, Curly suggests that Jeeter hang himself, and tries to paint the same rosy picture of people singing "sad songs" at his funeral as he does in *Oklahoma!* in "Pore Jud Is Daid."

It would have been foolhardy of Rodgers and Hammerstein to have failed to use ideas in the original play that could *serve* their musical. However, one of the major causes of failure of the original play was the haphazard use of folk songs that were included because characters were made to ask someone to sing them! In the party scene (Scene 4 of the play), there are five such songs: two "crowd" songs and one each sung by Old Man Peck, Curly, and Ado Annie. None has anything at all to do with the play.

On the other hand, the songs in *Oklahoma!* grew out of the characters and the situations.

Will Parker, a young man named once in the play but

created by Hammerstein, has just returned from Kansas City where he won a roping contest. (He wants to marry Ado Annie and now has the $50—the prize money—that her father requires him to have if he is to consent to the marriage.) Will (with the crowd's assistance) sings "Everything's Up to Date in Kansas City," in which he details the latest inventions in an amusing way.

Later in the same scene, after a small reprise of "The Surrey with the Fringe on Top," Ado Annie has her comedy song, "I Cain't Say No," that tells of her hopeless inability to deny her kisses to any fellow who wants them. Later, Laury is made jealous of Curly, who is reportedly courting another girl, and she sings a charm song, "Many a New Day," that says she won't blubber "if her man goes away," but that she will "start all over again."

The Peddler has one song after he has tried quietly to seduce Ado Annie, but is overheard by her father, who is willing to let him proceed but insists on marriage or else.

The next song in the scene is a "charm" duet between the hero and heroine, "People Will Say We're in Love." It pivots on the word "don't"—"throw bouquets," "please my folks," "laugh at my jokes," etc.—and is an oblique love song. It leads to the hero's asking Laury to break her date with the psychotic Jud and go instead with Curly to the party. But Laury declines because of the unpleasant dream she has had that Jud might harm Curly.

I have already alluded to the next two songs, "Pore Jud Is Daid" and "Lonely Room," which help establish Jud as a human being to be pitied.

Next, Laury meets her girlfriends, who want to know if she really plans to go to the "social" with Jud. She says she will tell them her plans when she can "think ever'thin' out clear." This begins "Out of My Dreams," a light waltz that becomes Laury's unhappy dream of Jud killing Curly (a ballet). On awakening, Jud is present to escort her as she looks "wistfully back at Curly." Act I ends.

Act II begins with a rousing chorus, "The Farmer and the Cowhands Should Be Friends." All the folks are enjoying the picnic. This is followed by a melodramatic sequence—in the bidding for Laury's basket, Curly, by selling all of his worldly possessions (horse, saddle, and gun) is finally able to outbid Jud. Meanwhile, Ado Annie and Will Parker get back together with "All or Nuthin'."

Curly and Laury are to be married, and a group song commences with "They couldn't pick a better time to start in life!" which is the beginning of the title song. All of the advantages of life in the Oklahoma Territory are extolled.

After the death of Jud and the exoneration of Curly, the show ends with a reprise of "Oh, What a Beautiful Morning."

There are thirteen different songs (not counting reprises) in *Oklahoma!*

In Frank Loesser's *Guys and Dolls*, there are sixteen songs *plus* several reprises. They are set up briefly as follows:

"Fugue for Tinhorns" (trio) establishes the fact that the show is about gamblers, in this case racehorse gamblers.

"Follow the Fold" is sung and played by the Mission Group. It sets them up as a hymn-singing, do-good group.

"The Oldest Established" (floating crap game) describes the plight of the crapshooters who are without a place to hold their next game.

"I'll Know" (when my love comes along) is a duet between Sky and Sister Sarah. She is outraged that he *obviously* wants to make love to her, and she describes exactly what she thinks her love will be like. He replies sarcastically.

"A Bushel and a Peck" is a nightclub entertainment song-and-dance for Miss Adelaide and the Hot-Box Dolls.

"Adelaide's Lament" is a comedy song in which Adelaide blames her pulmonary distresses on her failure to get Nathan to marry her after an engagement of fourteen years.

"Guys and Dolls" is a vaudeville number. Sung by two of the gamblers, it details the unfortunate men who are what would normally be considered good," but who must be defecting from *their* usual routines for some "doll."

"If I Were a Bell" (I'd be ringing) is sung by a drunken Sarah in Havana after a dinner at which she has been drinking milk with a "native flavoring" (rum). She is happy.

"My Time of Day" is Sky's short poetic song about the beautiful time before dawn that he knows so well but has never before spoken of to a "doll." This leads to—

"I've Never Been in Love Before," sung by Sky and Sarah, back in New York in front of the Mission, just after their trip to Havana. They are both happy.

Act I ends when the gamblers are flushed out of the Mission where they have been shooting craps, and Sarah believes Sky has taken her away so that they might have this opportunity.

Act II opens with—

"Take Back Your Mink," another entertainment song for Miss Adelaide and her Hot-Box Dolls. It provides an excuse for a simulated striptease.

"Adelaide's Second Lament" is the result of Nathan's standing her up (for a crap game) when she thought they were to have been married. Musically, it is a reprise of the first Lament, but has a different lyric.

"More I Cannot Wish You" (than to wish you find your love) is sung by Sarah's grandfather. He knows she is in love with Sky but that she is unwilling to admit it.

"Luck Be a Lady" is sung by Sky at a crap game prior to his purported single roll of the dice which he hopes will win him all the gamblers' attendance at Sarah's Mission (his part of their bargain).

"Sue Me" is a duet between Adelaide and Nathan in which she complains of his mistreatment of her, and he can only say "Sue me" and "I love you."

"Sit Down, You're Rockin' the Boat" is sung by one of the gamblers backed up musically by all the others at the crucial Mission meeting. It is a rousing "white spiritual."

"Marry the Man Today (and Change Him Tomorrow)" is sung by Adelaide and Sarah who have just made identical mistakes: they have dismissed their men before marrying them.

"Guys and Dolls" (reprise) is sung as a finale by the entire company, both couples having been happily married, as in "a fable," which is the subtitle of the show.

(The form of "Sue Me" is most unusual. It feels quite "natural" but it achieves both its dramatic and musical aims because of its regular contrasts. In a general way, the structure is *A B A B A B*; the release *(B)* and the *A* sections are all in the same key, but their movements are vastly different. This "movement" is derived from the two characters in this comical situation. The *A* is Adelaide's speedy complaint about Nathan's false promises. The *B* in each case is Nathan's slow response, admitting that her accusations are valid, but "I love you." Also, *B* has a sense of fumbling. The three *A*s are all in seventeen measures of 6/8 time. The first two *B*s are twelve bars in 3/4, four in 2/4, and fourteen in 3/4; the final *B* consists of eight slow 3/4 bars. "Sue Me" is an extraordinary example of a composer's translating literally a dramatic situation and the opposing reactions of two characters—accusation and defense—into a rational musical form.)

Of the many examples of original placement of songs (a duet in this case), none is more original than "You Must Meet My

Wife," in Stephen Sondheim's *A Little Night Music*. In Act I, Scene 4, the hero Fredrik, a middle-aged man, visits his former mistress Desiré, an actress, in her hotel. He has deposited his very young and—after a year of marriage—still virginal wife at their home and "gone out for a breath of fresh air." He has not seen Desirée for fourteen years. Quite obviously, Fredrik has called on Desirée with hopes of having sexual relations. It is my own feeling that a less thoughtful composer than Sondheim would have given Fredrik a song that might have said that he had always been in love with her, his former mistress —this would have been one way of setting about his present wooing of her. However, that is, thankfully, *not* what Sondheim did. Quite oppositely, he wrote a song on a subject that might have seemed, under the circumstances, altogether taboo: his young wife. The song develops comically as a duet. Fredrik is sincere in enumerating his wife's good qualities, while Desirée is sarcastic. After the duet, Fredrik fumbles: he is unable to say precisely why he has come to see his old friend, but she answers the question:

"Of course. What are old friends for?"

What I feel has happened here is that the unexpected has been amusingly musicalized while the expected has been made short shrift of by a single and charming line of dialogue.

Another example of the unexpected happens in *A Chorus Line*, when the toughest and most supercilious of the girls begins a song of warm remembrance (that is taken up by two other girls in a dreamlike mood), "At the Ballet" (lyrics by Edward Kleban), in which she recalls her dreary childhood and her escape from its unpleasant reality "at the ballet."

It is essential that writers discover new, unexpected though understandable subject matter and positioning of songs in their shows. The best musicals of the past thirty years had to face similar problems in breaking away from shows that preceded theirs. The creators of the "new" shows (1940–1970) solved their own problems. Now, once again, it is necessary for contemporary musical-theatre creators to examine their material more closely in order to discover newer placements and newer subjects. The now-older ones cannot be reused. New becomes old with repeated use.

4

Assignments

The following are the four first "exercises" I assign members of my BMI Musical Theatre Workshops. All four of the plays involved are to be found in *Best Plays, Series Three*, edited by John Gassner (Crown).

I urge the studious reader to undertake these assignments only after carefully reading the preceding sections. All four assignments should be executed as though *this* particular song were part of an entire score, not an incidental song. The writer should read each play in its entirety before undertaking each assignment because only in this way can he hope to be able to particularize the character who is to sing the song. Also, only after considering the play as a whole, will he be able to evaluate the situation assigned.

Also, he must not—either intentionally or accidentally—employ in the lyrics of his song, facts, incidents, "color," or point of view about a character that has not as yet been divulged at the moment in the play where the song occurs.

For example, in *A Streetcar Named Desire* the song assigned to Blanche Dubois should not suggest her ultimate deterioration, for this is to emerge or be implied bit by bit during subsequent scenes. Also, because Blanche is alone with Mitch, and is to sing a ballad (in this assignment), there will be a temptation to write "romantic" lyrics—some kind of love song involving these two characters. This temptation must be resisted, since at this point in the play Mitch has not considered Blanche in this light and Blanche's romantic sights—real or imaginary—are set far higher than Mitch.

The question, then, is: what *could* the song be about? There are many choices. It could concern Blanche's present plight or consist of invented material—not necessarily articulated in the play itself but consistent with what has been written—about Blanche's earlier life.

For the lyricist, the language should conform to the character and the style of the dialogue she speaks. It should represent the degree of her education, her special background, age, and speech patterns.

Occasionally, a character in a charged, emotional situation may conceivably transcend his ordinary speech patterns in the lyrics he sings. (Singing itself transcends reality.) Examples of this uncharacteristic expression may be cited:

"My Time of Day" *(Guys and Dolls)*
"Soliloquy" *(Carousel)*
"The Bench Scene" *(Carousel)*

The plays assigned here may not (probably *would* not) lend themselves to treatment as musicals, a fact which makes these assignments more difficult, but that is one reason they are given—to make the participant think more clearly and work harder.

All five assignments have built-in restrictions and limitations, which should also help sharpen the writer's thinking, so in this sense, the boundaries are helpful. Similarly, the musical form—also restrictive—will be helpful in that the writer with dramatic inclinations cannot be self-indulgent, since he is required to express himself completely within specified limits.

The composer is urged *not* to consider coloring his music according to the time or place of the play's setting. Doing so will result in pastiche, which is itself another kind of limitation. Illustrations to support this point of view are abundant. Neither Mozart nor Rossini wrote Spanish music for *Don Giovanni* or *The Barber of Seville*. Alban Berg did not write music of the Napoleonic period in *Wozzeck*. Richard Strauss wrote his own music for *Salome*, set in biblical days; for *Elektra*, set six centuries earlier; and for *Der Rosenkavalier*, set in the eighteenth century.

The same applies to word styles. T. S. Eliot did not imitate twelfth-century English in *Murder in the Cathedral;* nor did Jean Anouihl, when writing *Becket*. Archibald MacLeish wrote in *his* own style when he penned *J. B.*, his verse-drama about the biblical Job.

Painters also did not refer to ethnic or historical or anthropological sources when they painted. Rembrandt's *Descent from the Cross* is costumed in the painter's own time. The many early Italian (Medieval and Renaissance) painters who made canvases pertaining to the life of Jesus, or of later saints and martyrs, employed castles of their own times as backgrounds and costumes that they themselves wore.

Finally, Richard Rodgers did not write a Siamese musical in *The King and I*, nor did Harnick and Bock write a turn-of-the-century Polish musical in *Fiddler on the Roof.*

Be yourselves. See the characters and situations through your own eyes. Be innocent of travel folders and aware only of universal people in any time and place.

In truth, all imitation without comment is pointless. First, pure imitation cannot equal what was actually written in a particular period; therefore, *imitation* must betray itself as a "second-best" copy. If pastiche contains a kind of built-in comment, a point of view about the period or style which it evokes, in a sense it can become a contemporary piece. When "comment" is not intended—a condition which characterizes the majority creative point of view—the composer more usually composes music in his own style and leaves the period or place (when they are not his own) to the scenic designer, the costumer, or simply to an announcement in the program.

Good musical examples exist in Prokofiev's *Classical* Symphony which *suggests* works of Mozart and Haydn but could only have been written by Prokofiev in his own time. Also, Leonard Bernstein lampooned all operatic "jewel songs" (*Faust* in particular) in "Glitter and Be Gay" in *Candide;* however, this is Bernstein, not a copy of Gounod.

ASSIGNMENT I

Write a *ballad* for Blanche Dubois in Tennessee Williams' play, *A Streetcar Named Desire,* near the end of Scene 3. Blanche is disturbed on seeing her sister Stella become reconciled with her husband Stanley following a violent argument. She runs downstairs where she encounters Stanley's friend, Mitch, who attempts to pacify her.

As this is the first assignment, I will again call attention to several built-in pitfalls:

Blanche is not (as yet) feeling romantic about Mitch; Blanche is not (as yet) showing symptoms of losing her mind.

Subject matter for lyrics cannot be drawn from what has *not* yet happened in the play. Very little has actually happened, but the creative lyricist also has, in addition to the play's action up to this point, all of Blanche's past life—real or imagined—to draw on.

Remember: the assignment is a *ballad*. It is a solo (not a duet). The writer must create a layout which might (if desired), include spoken dialogue during a repetition of part of the song. This can come literally from the play or be created for this purpose. Nothing in the lyrics should be repeated from the play *if* it is also to be spoken. Since the song occurs near the end of the scene, it is stronger for the scene end, if the song actually closes the scene.

Remember, also, a play—produced, filmed, published, and so on— is frozen. If it is to be used as basis for a libretto (explained in another part of this book) it is subject to change.

The ballad's refrain (apart from its verse) should be in *A A B A* form. In fact, this form should be adhered to as a matter of discipline in all assignments.

ASSIGNMENT II

Write a *charm song* for Frankie at any point in Carson McCullers' play *A Member of the Wedding*. Remember what a charm song is, what its spirit and mood are. Think carefully about the character of Frankie—how she speaks, how her manner of speaking is unique, and how your song relates to, or is a part of, the situation for which you choose to write it.

ASSIGNMENT III

Write a *comedy song* for Lola in William Inge's play *Come Back, Little Sheba*, remembering that she appears foolish to us but that, in reality, she is pathetic.

For reference, see "Adelaide's Lament" *(Guys and Dolls)* and "I Can't Say No" *(Oklahoma!)*.

ASSIGNMENT IV

Write a musical scene near the end of Arthur Miller's *Death of a Salesman*, starting after the exit of Willie Loman's wife,

131

Linda, and ending abruptly on the crash of Willie's car.

Remember, you are not writing grand opera but a musical show. Use Willie as the central figure. Carefully analyze his mood at this point. Note the change (without transition) to the triumphant football game of years before. I suggest the use of spoken dialogue for Ben and the occasional calls from Linda. The music should be continuous and, although it is guided by the dramatic situation which contains many brief and sudden shifts, the scene as a whole must have *form* which, in my opinion, should probably come from the employment of a complete song sung by Willie, with echoes and variations of that song used as background music and perhaps at least part of a reprise of it before Willie's final exit.

One final exercise is recommended. It will require much thinking and little writing.

There are certain nouns that lyric writers have employed for centuries. They are almost inevitable, since they represent much of what we see. However, they have become clichés— not in themselves but with the modifiers (adjectives, usually) that writers have chosen to use with them. For example, the easiest first non-idea anyone can copy is "blue skies," or "soft white clouds." There have to be many other modifiers that will prevent their sounding tired. Often, it is the use of one of these nouns in a phrase or clause that bedraggles them.

The following will illustrate some of the infinite possibilities of freshness that can be created to keep these nouns alive. All of these examples are taken from poems by Emily Dickinson (1830–1886):

> drip with sunset
> proudest trees
> The day came slow

I send two sunsets
  Day and I——
When winds take forests in their paws
I'll tell you how the sun rose—
  A ribbon at a time—
The hours slid fast—as hours will
Dipping birds
And then he [a bird] drank a Dew
From a convenient Grass.
I know a place where summer strives
Handsome skies
The moon is distant from the sea
—Miles of sparks—at evening—
—my now bewildered dove
We should not mind so small a flower—

As most of these little excerpts are more than a century old, no contemporary lyricist would copy their precise imagery, but they do suggest myriad other possibilities.

As an exercise, I suggest that the new lyricist surround the following common nouns with as many fresh phrases as possible. These particular words, and many others like them, will come up again and again during lyric-writing. Use them in singular or plural:

sky	star
cloud	river
earth	stream
tree	hair
flower	eyes
rose	sunrise
moon	sunset
shadow	

I defined earlier the $A\,A\,B\,A$ form which is indeed the basis of form in all Western music and indicated that I would give a list of exceptions to this form. Because such a list would be limitless, the following is only peripheral. However, the reader must note that, though the examples do deviate from the precisely regular form, even these deviations rely on the basic structure by retaining the eight-bar balance or its equivalent feeling.

"Tea for Two" (Caesar and Youmans) $A\,B\,A$ plus a coda (tailpiece, or ending, of eight more bars).

"I Guess I'll Have to Change My Plans" (Dietz and Schwartz) A^1A^2 (first two bars begin with the original theme, then develop away from repetition), B (four bars, against the two preceding eight-bar sections), A (four bars)! [$A(8)$ A(8-developing) $B(4)$ $A(4)$].

"Dancing in the Dark" (Dietz and Schwartz) $A(16)$ A(16 going into an ending).

"You're the Top" (Porter) A(16 bars) A(16 bars with minor alteration).

"Begin the Beguine" (Porter) $A(16)$ $A(16)$ $B(16)$ $A(16)$ $C(16)$ $C(16)$ coda (12). Although the B section sounds like a release because of key change, and C serves as an intensification of the song, *all* the material is taken from the original A and changes only as it flows up and down melodically.

"You'll Never Walk Alone" (Rodgers and Hammerstein) is in blocks of eight bars, but contains development without repetition. It always progresses dramatically and harmonically. There are four eight-bar "blocks" and a four-bar coda or "wind-down."

"I Could Have Danced All Night" (Lerner and Loewe) is in sixteen-bar blocks, all made from the same material.

There is almost no repetition. After A(16) and A(16), which is a development, there is B(16), which is different from the two A sections only because it goes through a succession of key changes, and A(16), which contains elements of the original A, but these are expanded.

"Make Someone Happy" (Comden-Green and Styne) A (16) and A(24). The elongated second A begins as a repetition of the first A but develops and includes an extended ending.

"Sunrise, Sunset" (Bock and Harnick) A(8) B(8) A(8) B(8).

"I Loved You Once in Silence" (Lerner and Loewe) A(16) A(16) B(8) A(11) coda (10). The third A section breaks off suddenly, and, after a pause, the coda winds up the song.

"America" (Sondheim and Bernstein) from *West Side Story* A(10) B(10) A(10).

"Something's Coming" (Sondheim and Bernstein) Vocal introduction, four bars (repeated), followed by A(12) B (10), both repeated (this is in the verse). The refrain is made of the same material as A of the verse: A(12) B(10) C (serves actually as the release—32 bars) A(12) B(10) C (16) A(14). To recapitulate: Verse A(12), B(10), Refrain A (12), B(10), C(32), A(12), B(10), C(16), A(14). B of the verse is also made of an elongated note value version of B of the verse.

How does one account for these deviations and the many others not listed here? The simple and only answer that I can give is that the writers were able to achieve a sense of balance that in these cases worked. However, I again urge the student to restrict himself at first to the simple $A A B A$ form. It not only works, but the restriction it necessitates works superbly, not only of itself, but as an exercise. If anyone—student or master—can say everything he wishes or has to say within the regular form, he has indeed achieved a difficult goal.

Four Essays

DREAMING

ONE OF THE WORST epithets frequently applied to an adaptation of a musical play, book, or film for use as a libretto is that the result is "faithful to the original." Usually this is meant as a compliment, but the appraiser has then incorrectly concluded that Rodgers and Hammerstein, let us say, had merely *inserted* their songs into the book of Molnar's *Liliom* when they transformed the play into *Carousel.* Or that da Porte and Mozart had only *musicalized* Beaumarchais' *Marriage of Figaro.* Or that Boito and Verdi had merely vocalized Shakespeare's *Othello.* The list of adaptations employed in popular as well as in "serious" musical theatre is endless. In any case, when the new product has really worked, the changes (discussed previously) have been significant.

Actually, a theatregoer who says, in what is intended as

adverse criticism, that Stephen Sondheim and Hugh Wheeler had *not* been faithful to Ingmar Bergman's film *Smiles of a Summer Night*, is at least perceptive, for what the writers had actually done to the original in translating it into this other medium—musical theatre—was to make it work by making it their own.

Shakespeare's characters and plots had already existed before he was born. They had been sometimes used several times before Shakespeare began to deal with them. But by endowing them with a new form, a fresh and viable dramatic structure, and sublime poetry, Shakespeare gave them a new identity.

When musical-theatre writers decide to adapt anything, it is essential that they consider the basic plot structure (story line) and then the characters which they are appropriating to themselves: How will the *present* writers use them? Does he need all of them, or would it be wise to dispose of some or perhaps add others, in order to bring his singing cast to life?

Most times—if we are to benefit from history—his musical will have to begin in a manner different from the original play. For example, in *The Most Happy Fella*, Frank Loesser introduced his heroine in a way that was better than that of the original Sidney Howard play, *They Knew What They Wanted*, by adding a scene for her ahead of the play's start. Further, in order to do this, he had to create a new character who could play that scene with her.

After the new first scene, it became evident that Loesser would need still another new scene in which the male protagonist, Tony, would be introduced—this, still prior to Act I of the play. In this second new scene, the audience sees something paralyzingly terrible happen—Tony asks a photographer to take a picture of his handsome young foreman, Joey, which he ostensibly wants as a memento when Joey leaves.

We, the audience, know that Tony plans to enclose this photograph in a letter to Rosabella, his bride-to-be, claiming it to be of himself. We watch in dismay as the picture is being taken, cringing because we realize that when Rosabella eventually arrives to marry Tony, she will be shocked, incredulous, and horrified by Tony's duplicity. We would like to prevent his sending the picture, but we can only watch and then witness the inevitable, needlessly distressing result.

Loesser's "opening up" of the original play in this manner was well conceived. What we are now *shown* was, in the Howard version, *told* to the audience *after the fact*, and therefore it was much less forceful that when presented in Loesser's dramatic fashion.

I could refer to many other similar examples, but this one will suffice. However, by showing this one, another and different point presents itself: the audience—except in a mystery play—always knows *everything*. Only certain other characters in the play are not aware of some things and it is because of this fact that writers engender suspense.

For clarification of this idea, let me point to other similar examples. In *Othello*, Iago states his nefarious plans (to destroy Othello, Desdemona, and Cassio) and we know his reasons. But these three people who are to become his victims are unaware of his intentions and do not observe their progressive effects. At the very outset of *Romeo and Juliet*, the chorus relates the entire plot and its disastrous results. We know of Friar Laurence's plan to give Juliet a drug that will make her appear dead. However, he fails in his efforts to relay this information to Romeo so that he will be present in her crypt when she awakens. When Romeo hears of Juliet's "death," he hastens to her bier, regards her as dead, and takes his own life. Awakening and finding Romeo dead, Juliet also commits suicide.

In the best American musicals of the past, the audience has also known everything. At the end of the first act of *Carousel*, we know that Billy Bigelow plans to join his friend Jigger in staging a holdup. His wife Julie does not know of this, but she feels apprehensive. We know that Sky Masterson was not responsible for the crap game which Sarah sees ended by police and which she *thinks* Sky is responsible for—a misunderstanding that brings Act I of *Guys and Dolls* to an end. In *A Little Night Music*, we know that the *uninvited* couple will spend the weekend in the country with the invited couple and that there will be complications and unpleasantnesses.

My reason for titling this section "Dreaming" was that I had in mind the adaptor's method of arriving at these all-important situations and the precise nature of the characters who fill them out. For in the best musicals and operas—in the past, the present, and hopefully in the future—as long as librettists continue to work with adaptations, librettist and lyricist must learn to dream.

To be more explicit, I recently encountered a situation that called for dreaming up an entire parade of things that did not exist in original source material. One writer, at work (an exercise) on a musical based on Booth Tarkington's *Alice Adams*, was continually running out of material because what he needed was not present in Tarkington's book. What was absent was sufficient detail. Finally I asked a question which set him free of Tarkington: what did Alice do with her time? She had no occupation; her interests seemed limited only to pretending that she and her family were socially and financially better off than they actually were and trying to "win" a desirable, socially and financially superior young man.

"What," I asked, "does Alice do with the vast amount of time she must pass in doing nothing seven days and nights every week? Does she have any interests or hobbies or plans?"

I suggested that he stop referring back to Tarkington's novel and "dream" for himself what Alice could possibly fill her life with.

This suggestion proved helpful. He invented for Alice an

ambition to write screenplays. This invented ambition took her to the movies every afternoon when the admission price was lowered and when she would be less likely to be noticed by the town gossips. In this way (not perhaps the only or best solution to a major problem, but *one* solution for eliminating a vacuum), the writer was able to take a more positive approach toward making the *character* of Alice a bit more meaningful and interesting.

In another case, a lyricist wrote a song in which the singing character was advising his friend, who was New York-bound to try to build a career for himself, about his future. The words I read sounded like a sophomoric pep talk. All of the images were general and passé. The words were dull because they were nonspecific and, in the end, travelled nowhere.

I asked the question: "If your best friend were going away in this manner and wanted your advice, would you be so impotent to help him that you'd simply offer encouragement that lacked specific recommendations, suggestions, warnings?"

The answer, of course, was "No."

The new lyrics were specific, and the end result was a successful comedy song that reminded me somewhat of Polonius' advice to his son Laertes in *Hamlet*, when Laertes was departing for school in France. In that speech, Polonius not only employs a great many specifics but, in having him so, Shakespeare gave Polonius' character another dimension. When Polonius appears again later on in the play, he is "preclothed": we now *expect* his loquaciousness that was established in the earlier scene.

This "dreaming," in my opinion, is not to be underestimated by any writer, particularly a writer of adaptations. It can create situations where none previously existed. It can enlarge the dimensions of characters that were originally too limited and circumscribed. It can open up to the lyricist ideas which might also have been limited in the original material. To librettist, lyricist, and composer, "dreaming" can find positions for songs so that they will not become too expected and too much a part of the conventional tried-and-true that can only lead to dullness.

Theatre is action and feeling and poetry and music and reality seen through unreality. Schiller's play *Mary Stuart* is bigger and far more interesting than history. If one wants history, he does not rely on Shakespeare's *Richard II, Richard III, Henry IV, Henry V, Henry VI* or *Henry VIII* for all the facts and nothing but the facts. He must consult other sources. For the theatre is not and never will be interested in facts; at its very best, it changes them at will to suit the needs of the creative artist, who alters them to accommodate his own purposeful dreams.

"Dreaming" will give proper creative impetus to the writer, lyricist, and composer. Disciplined technique will do the rest.

PRODUCTION VALUES

The writer of a musical show must have, among many other things, a physical vision of what he writes: he must "see" it on the stage and attempt at least to feel what the audience's response will be. It is certainly true that when or if his show is actually put on the stage, its look will be considerably altered by the interpretive talents of the stage director and his collaboration with scenic and costume designers. Nevertheless, the writer's initial vision must have existed first for *any* subsequent vision to be possible. By now—nearly four centuries later—Shakespearean plays have undergone and will continue to undergo many physical metamorphoses—alterations in place and time. His "Street in Verona" and "Another Part of the Forest" have on occasion become abstract or stylized, or pinpointed as "New York" or any other place in, or absent from, the world. What matters is that the plays continue to work despite most of these external transformations, for in their original presentations there was *no* scenery, *no* lights, and few if any costumes that differed from the ordinary dress of Shakespeare's own time. Against this "limitation," in his dialogue, Shakespeare of necessity had to particularize place and at least time of day, if not of period. He did not try to conceal the paucity of his stage, a fact which must have been all too obvious, but instead pointed it out! There is no more eloquent example of this than the opening lines (Prologue) of *Henry V*, in which the speaker asks:

> Can this cockpit hold the vast fields of France? or may we cram
> Within this wooden O the very casques
> That did affright the air at Agincourt?
>
> And let us . . .
> On your imaginary forces work
>
> Piece out our imperfections with your thoughts
>
> Think, when we talk of horses, that you see them
> Printing their proud hoofs i' the receiving earth;
> For 'tis your thoughts that now must deck our kings
>
> Turning the accomplishment of many years
> Into an hour-glass [etc.]. . . .

Beginning at about the turn of the present century, the American musical theatre found itself at the opposite end of this clear, clean spectrum that called upon the audience's imagination. About 1900, none was needed. The stages were packed with scenery as realistic and elaborate as the techniques of the day allowed. This realism grew. By about 1920, when Ziegfeld and his various competitors were mounting their *Follies, Vanities,* and other revues, it was the eye that was busied while the audience's mind with its potentially fantastic imagination was allowed to stultify.

History continues to repeat itself. They "went about as fer

as they could go" and ended in repetition like a broken phonograph record, boring, and finally losing, their audience. We were then back for a time to unvarnished simplicity.

The musical theatre by now has passed through a period of semi-stylization and now has rediscovered the values of the audience's imagination. Those people out front do not fall prostrate on the floor with shock because they are shown shifting scenery which allows a more fluid production. And in order for this to happen, scenery had to be more skeletal. Lighting almost imperceptibly began to grow in importance in limiting or expanding a scene.

John Dexter, the superb English director, made audiences hold their breaths in fear as a Spanish army, in single file and holding hands, passed perilously around a narrow ledge in the Andes *(The Royal Hunt of the Sun)*, and yet there was no attempt at *showing* height or narrowness: we were simply *told* that it was there.

The same director, in the more recent *Equus* by the same author of *Royal Hunt* (Peter Schaffer), employed a set consisting of a rectangular wooden stage circumscribed with bannisters and practical entryways on all sides. The play itself, the director, the actors, and the lighting, made the audience see quite clearly a psychiatrist's office, a stable, a meadow, a beach, a home, a moviehouse, a store, and many other places that were nevertheless not at all physically represented.

Boris Aronson has been successful again and again in what he has provided, expecially for two of Stephen Sondheim's musicals (directed by Harold Prince)—*Company* and *A Little Night Music*. In the latter, there is a permanent background for each of the two acts. Small pieces of scenery slide on and off, defining bedrooms, theatres, dining rooms, gardens, and many other places. The old ceiling has disappeared, as have the walls. When the actor believes he is knocking at a door, we do not notice that his knuckles only strike the air: he defines the nonexistent door for us and, without question, we accept it as fact.

Still later, in *A Chorus Line*, there is no scenery. The songs, monologues, and dances, with the invaluable definition of the lyrics (Edward Kleban), describe homes, theatres, schools, and the like. The singing-dancing actors, under the brilliant leadership of Michael Bennett, lead us where and how we are to go.

I began this brief section with a statement that the writer must have a physical vision, and so he must. The details of this vision may be considerably altered, implemented , and even improved upon as the show reaches the stage. Good! But, to repeat, without the initial vision that works for the writer as he creates, there will be nothing for anyone else to build on.

REGARDING THE USE OF COPYRIGHTED MATERIAL

Since musical theatre, now and in the past, has nearly always largely depended for libretto ideas and bases on material that was initially created for other media—plays, films, novels, short stories, and ideas in other forms—it follows that much of the most desirable material is protected by copyright.

In our own time, we recall a few successful musical adaptations based on "public domain" stocks. (For the uninitiated, works that are now in "public domain" are either very old ones or those that are old enough to have survived the length of their copyrights.) Among these are *Man of La Mancha*, based on Cervantes' *Don Quixote; Oliver*, based on Charles Dickens' *Oliver Twist; Two Gentlemen of Verona*, based on Shakespeare's play; *Your Own Thing*, based on Shakespeare's *Twelfth Night; West Side Story*, based on the same author's *Romeo and Juliet;* and *Candide*, based on Voltaire's work. Nearly all of the other most successful works have been adapted from material that was written and copyrighted within the past fifty years, most of it even much later.

On the other hand, composers and lyricists in the higher echelon have, at the start of their careers, written many shows that were never produced, and then others that they were able to see in amateur presentations. Even their first major productions that were hits never assured anyone that everything afterward would enjoy the same kind fate. For example, Jerome Kern (*Show Boat, Roberta,* and many others) had twenty-one shows produced between 1910 and 1920. Of these, five had fewer than fifty performances, five others had fewer than one hundred, six others had fewer than one hundred fifty, and the others were hits: five out of twenty-one shows were big hits.

Rodgers and Hart had their first hit with the 1925 *Garrick Gaities.* Between 1930 and 1940, they were represented by nine Broadway shows. All these had substantial runs, but the many shows prior to 1925 were in the amateur category—learning pieces.

Sigmund Romberg (*Desert Song, The Student Prince, Blossom Time, The New Moon,* and so on) had twenty-four productions between 1920 and 1930. Of these, six had fewer than one hundred showings. Cole Porter, who wrote fewer shows than any of the other superwriters, had only eight shows produced between 1930 and 1940, only one of which flopped. George Gershwin, mostly in collaboration with his brother Ira, produced seventeen shows between 1920 and 1930. Six out of the seventeen fared poorly.

Beware of the writers who have their very first show produced on Broadway. In every such case—rare as it has been—its success (very rare) has been a fluke and has usually been followed by a big flop—and then silence.

That being the case, I think it highly unlikely that new writers' first, second, third, and even fourth creations of new musicals are going to merit or achieve production. I therefore cannot agree with the idea that new writers should apply for options giving them permission to use copyrighted material for a limited time, since they must pay for the privilege of working with it. Even if they succeed in buying such options (at perhaps $1,000 for a year's exclusive permission to work on a property), they will certainly not write it and sell it for production and get it on the stage during that one year. And so the renewals will be an additional cost (they could even be withheld), and then nothing may ever come of it. Indeed, the chances are that nothing *will* ever come of it!

I advise going ahead without permission. If what is written is sufficiently attractive and strong, and a first-rate producer options *it*, he will take options on the source material as well as on the musical version. Of course, there is always the risk that for one of many reasons the rights will truly not be available. That would certainly cause considerable frustration, but if the new writer is working on his first to fifth adaptation, I would advise his taking the chance.

I personally know at least three pairs of excellent, now-developed writers who have each "completed" three excellent shows to which they cannot get rights. One of these writers very recently had a great success and now his unproduced shows will all be seen. That, too, can happen.

I strongly urge new people, when they have "finished" a score based on their synopsized adaptation of a property, to begin work at once on a new project while their "finished" one is being shown about. The process of creation should never be interrupted for as long a period as is needed to market, prepare, rehearse, and see a show onto the stage. Besides, if the first good show is sold and produced, writers ought to be in a position to take advantage of whatever success they may have, to sail through now-open doors with other completed shows. I have also observed the pitiful waste of time and talent when that does not happen.

First things first, and the first consideration is to learn how to write shows and to practice writing shows until one that has distinction and *might* "work" has been created. After that, worry about "rights" and the many other nightmares between the manuscript and its realization on a stage.

PREPARING THE AUDITION OF A SHOW

If or when a score with a synopsis, or an entire musical replete with libretto, is finished, the writers will be eager—rightly or wrongly—to audition it for a producer, an agent, a director, or an experienced librettist. Before any move is made in this direction, there ought to be a number of auditions for other writers or any small group of people possessed of some knowledge about such things. The writers should try to observe *reactions* as opposed to "friendly" flattery. Listeners who know nothing whatsoever about shows are very apt to respond enthusiastically, and these reactions should be ignored. What you need is hard-core criticism. Do the songs sound as though they were composed circa 1940? Are the lyrics romantically June and moon, love and dove? Are the plot and theme old-fashioned?

Bear in mind this fact: very contemporary subjects have a way of going out of style before the writer's ink dries. Writing, marketing, financing, casting, rehearsing, and opening a musical show can well be a matter of three or four years, or at least two. The *newest* styles (compare them with ladies' dresses)—such as woman's lib, gay lib, the generation gap, treatment of minority groups, and many others—while they are still alive and active are nevertheless not to be used as an effective bandwagon that will drive the writers to instant attention and glory. After all, women's lib was treated in Aristophanes'

Lysistrata (fourth century B.C.) and Ibsen's *A Doll's House* (1879), but these were genuine works of art, and argument does not find its ideal pulpit in musicals. Treatment of black minorities was brought to general attention and elicited sympathy in *Uncle Tom's Cabin,* and the generation gap was made timeless in *Fiddler on the Roof.*

If and when you as writers decide that your "property" has genuine distinction, you will first try to interest an agent. If he truly believes in its merits, he will open doors to producers and directors. Following is some advice that this writer can offer you concerning what to do and what not to do at that time.

Good producers are eager to acquire good new works. They are also busy. The most experienced ones will want to read your book or a synopsis before hearing the music, because they have learned from experience that a score without a viable idea or book is like a disembodied spirit: it has no place to go, it doesn't exist totally, and, as a production, it will be heard by very few people.

If a producer or director likes the idea or the book, he will want to hear the "score"; however, this wish must not be construed literally. What he will really want to hear at first are a few of the most attractive songs.

Most producers very much resemble average audiences when it comes to music: they do not *know* great art but they know what they like. They will want to hear "tunes" first. These should be found in your ballads. Many producers, if taken with a tune, will want to hear it several times in order to find out for themselves whether or not they can remember it.

Next they will want to hear the comedy songs: are there laughs or pale, out-of-date attempts at being cute?

Most producers at this first audition will be willing to hear four, five, or six songs in all. *Do not begin a first audition at the beginning and hope to play the score in its entirety unless you are requested to do so.*

If the producer is titillated by what he hears (you will want to make a strong first impression), he will probably set up another appointment to hear the entire score and will probably bring several of his cohorts to listen with him and advise with him afterward.

Playing the songs (four or five) the first time or the second time (the entire score) is not quite enough. You need to narrate brief setups for each song—the situation that gives rise to it and the character who sings it. By all means avoid the use of proper names in these brief narratives.

Do *not* say: "Bill Haverland has decided not to marry Alice Jay because he believes he is in love with Dorothy Schmidlap, whose father, Joseph H. Schmidlap, is president of the Scranton National Bank."

The names will be confusing and will not be remembered. In this kind of narrative they are burdensome and irrelevant.

Rather say: the young leading man has changed his mind about the girl he is courting because he now fancies another girl who has a wealthy father.

Do not try to tell the entire plot when performing only a few songs. Instead, precede the audition, if possible, with a brief, well-planned summary, preferably only one paragraph, again avoiding proper names which generally confuse the hearer.

If the composer has a reasonably "acceptable" voice and good articulation, he may be entirely adequate for this kind of audition, both as pianist and singer. The lyricist then might introduce the show and the separate numbers. If the composer's voice is "unacceptable," one male and one female singer should be employed by the writers and rehearsed well in advance.

The question of sending or bringing taped scores is, in my

opinion, inadvisable if avoidable. If they are sent, no one may ever listen to them. I believe in any case that there is something too impersonal about tapes and that a live performance is in every way preferable.

If the producer decides to sign a contract or take an option for a period of time, he will want to have a series of backers' auditions, at which he will try to raise the necessary funds for financing the project. For this kind of performance, I think it is advisable to have perhaps two female and two male singers, attractive ones as well as appropriately good singers, with written verbal introductions committed to memory and still as brief as possible to avoid sprawling. Here, again, only the best songs should be used, and these should be presented in contrasting sequence: fast, slow, and so on. The general atmosphere ought to be as informal and relaxed as possible, and the presentations (not including the producer's introduction and his "pitch" to the audience afterward) should not exceed forty minutes or so. Once again, it is my advice *not* to try to present the entire score.

This final section will apply to only those very few writers who have had experience with the creation of several shows.

Perspective and honest self-judgment must be exercised carefully before approaching a producer or an agent with a new property, for if the property is thought to be less than interesting, the producer or agent may never again want to see anything else by the same writer.

One parting bit of advice: if you, the writer, are truly talented and serious, don't waste invaluable time trying to peddle an unpromising project when you might better work on another one. This business of peddling can not only be frustrating, but it can consume all of the writer's time and energy over a period of years, without any guarantee that the work will ever be produced; and all this while you will have no new or possibly better work in progress.

I know intimately two talented writers who wrote five or six excellent, if not world-shaking, songs for a well-known film scenario about ten years ago. On their own they have managed to meet the original author, have gotten to nearly all major producers, some agents, and even some potential backers, yet in those entire ten years they have had no positive success whatsoever. Today they are continuing hopefully to peddle their five or six songs, still knocking on doors and trying to make contacts. During this time, they could have written at least ten entire scores. What a waste!

Don't be guilty of wasting your time in this extravagant manner. There isn't *that* much time in anyone's life.

Index

Index

Bridge. *See* Relief
Brigadoon (Lerner-Loewe), 57, 59, 60, 82

Carousel (Rodgers-Hammerstein), 51, 63, 65, 139
  as adaptation, 78–79, 100
  love song in, 36
  synopsis of, 84–85
Characters
  in adaptations, 78–81
  development of, 32–33, 74–75, 116–117, 127–128
  song assignments for, 23–26
Charm songs, 13–15, 131
Chorus
  A A B A form in, 2
  and verse contrast, 4–6
Chorus Line, A (Kleban-Hamlisch), libretto for, 107, 108, 125
  opening of, 67
  staging of, 145
Clichés, in lyric writing, 132
Comedians (Griffiths), 107–108
Comedy, nature of, 58
Comedy of Errors (Shakespeare), 101
Comedy songs
  examples of, 56
  joke in, 55–56
  lyrics of, 15
  as plaints, 57–58, 131
  structure of, 59–60
Company (Sondheim), 33, 66–67, 107, 108
Consonant sounds, 53–54
Copyrighted material, 145
  buying options for, 147
Costume changes, timing for, 97

Desert Song, The (Romberg), 16, 35
Dexter, John, 144
Dickinson, Emily, 43–44, 132–133
"Do You Love Me?" (Harnick-Bock), 13, 37, 57–58

Equus (Shaffer), production of, 144
Euripides, 61

"Far From the Home I Love" (Harnick-Bock), 13, 41, 63
Farce, musicalization of, 102–103
Fiddler on the Roof (Harnick-Bock), 41, 44, 63
  as adaptation, 99–100
  opening of, 66
  songs in, 37, 57–58
"Friendship" (Porter), 40
Funny Thing Happened on the Way to the Forum, A (Sondheim-Shevelove), 36–37, 66, 102

Gassner, John, 127
Gershwin, Ira, 50–51
God's Favorite (Simon), 98–99
Green Grow the Lilacs (Riggs), 77, 78, 82–84
Griffiths, Trevor, 107–108
"Guess Who I Saw Today?" (Grand-Boyd), 42
Guys and Dolls (Loesser), 33, 51, 140
  ballads in, 11
  comedy song in, 56
  scene endings in, 118–119
  song placement in, 122–124

Hamlet (Shakespeare), 67–68, 69, 141
Hammerstein, Oscar, II, 54, 96
Harmonic idea, 20
Harmonic suspensiveness, 20, 21
Harmonization, 19
Harmony, 18
Henry V (Shakespeare), 143
History, adaptations from, 103–106
Hooks, in lyric endings, 41–42

"I Could Have Danced All Night" (Lerner-Loewe), 134
"If I Were a Rich Man" (Harnick-Bock), 44
Iphigenia in Aulis (Euripides), 61–62
"I've Grown Accustomed to Her Face" (Lerner-Loewe), 12–13, 36

Jokes, in comedy songs, 55–56, 59